TEACHING
MEASURES

ACTIVITIES, ORGANISATION AND MANAGEMENT

TEACHING MEASURES

ACTIVITIES, ORGANISATION AND MANAGEMENT

Janine Blinko and Ann Slater

Series Editor: Shirley Clarke

Hodder & Stoughton

A MEMBER OF THE HODDER HEADLINE GROUP

British Library Cataloguing in Publication Data

A catalogue entry for this title is available from the British Library

ISBN 0 340 63095 7

First published 1996
Impression number   10 9 8 7 6 5 4 3 2 1
Year   1999 1998 1997 1996

Typeset by Multiplex Techniques.
Printed in Great Britain for Hodder and Stoughton Educational, the educational division of Hodder Headline Plc, 338 Euston Road, London NW1 3BH, by The Bath Press, Avon.

CONTENTS

Introduction   viii

    Section A   Managing measurement: learning and teaching   1

1   **Developing a scheme of work for measurement**   2
2   **Planning for the teaching of measurement**   5
3   **The role of the teacher**   11

    Section B   Measurement activities   13

4   **Length**   14
    Introduction   15
    Activity 1 Beads   16
    Activity 2 Ten   18
    Activity 3 Sorting box   20
    Activity 4 How long?   23
    Activity 5 Plasticine sausages   25
    Activity 6 Bodies   27
    Activity 7 Detectives   30
    Activity 8 Make a line   32
    Activity 9 Metre mouse   35
    Activity 10 How high?   36
    Length activities for the rest of the class   38
    Photocopiable worksheets – Length   40

5   **Angle**   44
    Introduction   44
    Activity 1 Flowers   45
    Activity 2 Towers   47
    Activity 3 Turn!   48
    Activity 4 Letters   50
    Activity 5 Make two circles   51
    Activity 6 Doors   53
    Angle activities for the rest of the class   55
    Photocopiable worksheets – Angle   56

6 Mass   62

Introduction   62
Activity 1   Plasticine models   63
Activity 2   Envelopes   65
Activity 3   Filling boxes   67
Activity 4   Kilogram collections   69
Activity 5   Weigh yourself   71
Activity 6   Popcorn   74
Activity 7   How many stones?   76
Activity 8   Gravel balance   79
Activity 9   Magnets   82
Mass activities for the rest of the class   84
Photocopiable worksheets – Mass   86

7 Capacity/Volume   87

Introduction   88
Activity 1   Paint   89
Activity 2   Fill a pot   90
Activity 3   Sinkers   93
Activity 4   Junk boxes   95
Activity 5   Sponges   96
Activity 6   Blanket box   99
Activity 7   Body parts   102
Activity 8   Elastic bands   105
Activity 9   Fill a litre   107
Activity 10   200 grams of plasticine   111
Activity 11   Guess which box   113
Activity 12   Cones   114
Activity 13   Floor plans   116
Capacity/Volume activities for the rest of the class   117
Photocopiable worksheets – Capacity/Volume   119

8 Time   121

Introduction   121
Activity 1   Clock patience   122
Activity 2   Take your time   124
Activity 3   Modelling   125
Activity 4   Busy times   127
Activity 5   Time lines   128
Activity 6   Days of the week   130
Activity 7   A big clock   132
Activity 8   Jar lids   134
Activity 9   How long did it take   137
Activity 10   Digital display   138
Time activities for the rest of the class   140
Photocopiable worksheets – Time   142

9   Area   149

Introduction   149
Activity 1 Covering boxes   150
Activity 2 Body prints   153
Activity 3 Body measures   156
Activity 4 Cotton wool balls   158
Activity 5 Vegetables   161
Activity 6 Shadows   163
Activity 7 Boxes   165
Activity 8 Letter shapes   168
Activity 9 Grids   171
Activity 10 Make a square metre   173
Area activities for the rest of the class   176
Photocopiable worksheets – Area   178

Section C   Problems and investigations   182

10   Organising the problems in the classroom   183
11   Problems   184

Appendix   202

Glossary   210

INTRODUCTION

WHAT IS MEASUREMENT?

This is a tricky question. There are numerous facets to this aspect of mathematics, and consequently it needs a great deal of teaching time in the primary school. Piaget had firm views on when children are able to absorb the concepts necessary to understand different aspects of measure; instead of focusing on them, this book concentrates on two very different aspects of the teaching and learning of measurement: learning *how* to measure and *using* measurement.

Learning how to measure

Before measurement is really useful, children need to be able to understand what is being measured: Is it a space? Is it flat? Is it big? They also need to have had experiences which lead them to perceive that a measurement is conserved, no matter what its shape or orientation may be. The measurement of length and area are rather more straightforward than the others because they are more visible. Alongside these ideas is the development of an appreciation of the need to measure, and the need to measure with standard units*.

Once they appreciate these, they need to be able to make decisions about what tool(s) they should use to make the measurement, and what size unit to measure with. They also need to decide how accurate the measurement needs to be, develop the art of actually being able to measure accurately, and calculate if necessary. They also need to be able to answer questions like these:

- Where do you start to measure from on the ruler?
- What's that extra bit at the end for?
- Does it matter if I spill some water – should I wipe it up, or try to get it back in the jug?

Using measurement

Once children have the necessary understanding and skills, they need to use measurement in situations where the skill of meaning is almost incidental, and the problem becomes largely numerical – this, of course, is the aim. A simple example could be, 'When should I leave home to walk to the bus stop, to catch the 2.35 p.m. bus to the post office, and how much money do I need to take if I have three parcels to post when I get there?' There are lots of decisions to be made there, and lots of estimations too! Through open-ended problems the

* From Dickson, Browne and Gibson, *Children Learning Mathematics: A Guide to Recent Research*

children will start to develop a sophisticated understanding of the approximate nature of measurement.

It is worthwhile at this point to comment on estimation. In this book, we offer some activities that we have tried and enjoyed with children. There is no expectation that the children will always 'estimate first', which in reality, we did not find ourselves doing. Rather, the activities expect that children will develop an understanding of the need to estimate (which as adults we often do after the actual measurement, or at least simultaneously), and that they learn to answer and ask the question, 'Is that about right?' as they work.

HOW WE BELIEVE THAT CHILDREN LEARN MATHEMATICS BEST

Learning **how** to measure, and preparing children to be able to use measure as and when required has the potential of being a tedious process with pages of lines and pictures to measure. The following activities seem to make the children smile, and certainly have encouraged discussion with and between the children.

We believe that children learn best:

- when they enjoy it;
- when they are in control of the mathematics;
- when they know why they are doing it;
- when it is meaningful;
- when it is relevant;
- when their objectives are clear.

This particularly applies to their learning of measurement. We frequently underestimate how long children need/want to find practical solutions to measurement problems. The ability to 'visualise' and estimate quantities takes a great deal of time and requires a broad range of experiences. Children learn to measure best when they have this time and range.

WHAT IS IN THIS BOOK?

In this book, we offer a resource for measurement learning which addresses the current OFSTED criteria:

A sequence of carefully planned mathematical activities must be provided by teachers to ensure that basic skills are developed and used to the highest level of which each pupil is capable [...] The teaching should encourage the effective use of mathematics as a tool in a wide range of activities within the school and everyday life.

Handbook for Inspectors, Inspection Schedule Guidance, 1993

Our aims in writing this material were:

- to supply a comprehensive set of mathematics teaching and learning resources for teachers and children, in loose developmental order for measurement at Key Stages 1 and 2;
- to offer activities which give a clear indication of the learning focus taken from the National Curriculum Programmes of Study for 'Shape, Space and Measures' (SSM) and 'Using and Applying Mathematics' (UA). The objectives taken from the Programmes of Study are clearly shown in a box in each activity, and the direct reference to the National Curriculum is shown in the chart in the Appendix. We have chosen to identify the most important foci of the activities, rather than every possibility;
- to provide material which can be used in a scheme of work, and to offer clear guidance for the development of a scheme of work for measurement, incorporating direction for progression and continuity of activities;
- to provide material which is easy to use, and is suitably annotated and organised under clear headings to make it readable;
- to provide material which does not require the teachers to spend a great deal of time preparing worksheets, gameboards or other resources;
- to give clear guidelines for organising the measurement activities in the classroom, including what to do with the rest of the class. The teaching materials are offered in the comprehensive format shown in figure 1.

WHO IS THE BOOK FOR?

This book is essentially for primary school teachers, experienced or otherwise, and contains activities (and in some cases worksheets) for use by the children. It will also be of interest to co-ordinators of mathematics, student teachers, INSET providers, advisory teachers and teacher trainers.

HOW TO USE THIS BOOK

Teachers may choose to use this book in one of two ways:

- As a resource and guidance for the development of a scheme of work for measurement. In the Management section (see page 1), teachers will find a series of clearly described INSET activities to support this. You don't have to begin at the start of this section; you can slot in at an appropriate stage, if you are already part of the way through the process of developing a school scheme of work.

- As a reference for curricular activities in loose developmental order.

TITLE

┌──── LEARNING/TEACHING OBJECTIVES ────┐
│   │
│   │
└───────────────────────────────────────┘

What you will need

This section lists resources teachers will need to make available for the children.

What to do

This section describes the activity, the children's role in it and the teacher's role in it.

Organisation

This section describes the possible classroom organisation which will support the activity.

Activities that some children might need to do first

This section gives very brief descriptions of activities and/or directs teachers to other activities elsewhere in the book.

Reinforcing activities that some children might need

This section gives some very brief descriptions of activities and/or directs teachers to consolidation activities elsewhere in the book.

Activities that some children might be ready to move on to

This section describes extension activities and/or directs teachers to activities elsewhere in the book.

Similar activities for other measures

This section translates the original activity into a similar one which is directed at other areas of measure.

FIGURE 1 *Activity format*

SECTION

MANAGING MEASUREMENT: LEARNING AND TEACHING

This section gives guidance for whole school planning. It aims to support schools as they develop a scheme of work for the teaching and learning of measurement. We include suggestions for INSET activities and suggest ways to support the planning for progression and continuity in measurement. There is no time span placed on these INSET sessions – different schools will respond to them in different ways. It is not expected that they will each take the same amount of time, or that only one can be tackled in any one session.

CHAPTER

DEVELOPING A SCHEME OF WORK FOR MEASUREMENT

The purpose of this first chapter is twofold. Firstly, to develop an initial structure for the development of a scheme of work for measure, and secondly, to give the teachers involved an opportunity to become familiar with the requirements of the National Curriculum at Key Stage 1 and Key Stage 2 for measurement.

INSET 1: identifying National Curriculum Programme of Study statements

Staff work in twos or threes to concentrate on each of the aspects of measurement and identify which Programme of Study statements relate to each type of measure. The outcome of this could be presented as shown in figure 2. The text in italics takes phrases from the Programme of Study for Shape, Space and Measures at Key Stage 1.

	Length	Capacity/Volume	Mass	Time	Angle	Area
Key Stage 1	*For example:* • *comparison* • *non-standard* • *standard* • *estimation* • *use of instruments and scales*					
Key Stage 2						

FIGURE 2 *INSET 1 chart 'identifying statements'*

The next stage needs to build on the outcomes of INSET 1, by enlarging on the statements listed in the chart.

INSET 2: expanding and clarifying National Curriculum statements

Staff work in twos or threes to concentrate on each of the aspects of measurement. They should take each of the statements in turn and enlarge upon the meaning of them, and place them in loose developmental order, as in figure 3.

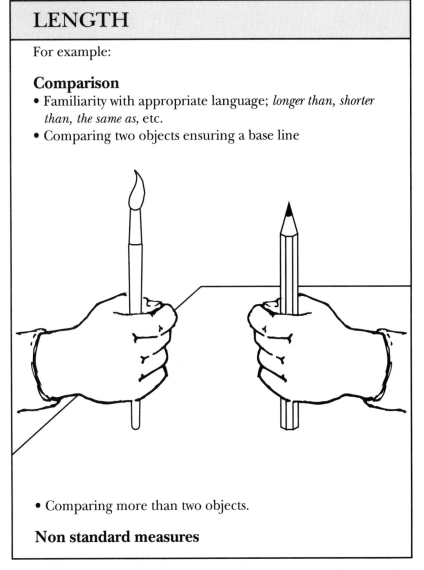

LENGTH

For example:

Comparison
- Familiarity with appropriate language; *longer than, shorter than, the same as*, etc.
- Comparing two objects ensuring a base line

- Comparing more than two objects.

Non standard measures

FIGURE 3   *INSET 2 chart to show developmental order*

Once the staff are agreed on their interpretation of the statements from the National Curriculum Programmes of Study, these need to be linked with activities.

INSET 3: making links with particular activities

Staff work in twos or threes on each of the aspects of measurement. Use the completed chart from INSET 2 (see figure 3), and either use the activities which follow to assign activities to each of these statements or use the chart in figure 4 as a guide and edit it accordingly. Activities are linked to the National Curriculum. See Appendix. With this task complete, the school now has a scheme of work for measurement.

LENGTH	ACTIVITIES
For example: **Comparison** • Familiarity with appropriate language; *longer than, shorter than, the same as*, etc. • Comparing two objects ensuring a base line • Comparing more than two objects. **Non standard measures**	*Beads* *Sorting box* *Bodies*

FIGURE 4 *INSET 3 chart to allocate appropriate activities*

CHAPTER 2

PLANNING FOR THE TEACHING OF MEASUREMENT

This section suggests an approach for taking the scheme of work and putting it into practice. We look at different levels of planning - whole school, year group and classroom - and suggest a series of INSET sessions which will take the scheme of work into the classroom.

1 WHOLE SCHOOL PLANNING

This activity assumes that schools have a complete scheme of work for measurement in a similar format to the one suggested previously.

INSET 4: deciding what will be taught when

KEY STAGE 1	Pre-Year 1	Year 1	Year 2
Length	For example: **Comparison** • Familiarity with appropriate language; *longer than, shorter than, the same as*, etc. • *Beads/Sorting box/Bodies*		
Capacity/Volume			
Mass			
Time			
Angle			
Area			

FIGURE 5 *INSET 4 Chart to allocate time*

Staff work in twos or threes on one or two of the aspects of measurement. Using the table in figure 5, ask the groups to 'cut and paste' statements from a copy of the scheme of work into what they consider to be the appropriate column. As a staff, check the balance of activities for each year; do likewise for Key Stage 2 in years 3-6.

It is expected that there will be substantial overlap between Key Stages and between year groups, and that teachers will envisage a need to 'revisit' particular aspects of measurement throughout the year.

2   YEAR GROUP PLANNING

If there is more than one teacher in each year group, those teachers need to work together to plan the year in terms of the teaching of measurement. The completed chart from INSET 4 (figure 5) will be needed in the next session.

INSET 5: planning the year

Using the part of the chart applicable to the year concerned, 'cut and paste' the information again, into the planning table shown in figure 6. Check the outcomes to ensure that sufficient resources will be available as and when children need them.

	AUTUMN TERM		SPRING TERM		SUMMER TERM	
Length				For example: **Comparison** • Familiarity with appropriate language; *longer than, shorter than, the same as,* etc. • *Beads/Sorting box/Bodies*		
Capacity/ Volume						
Mass						
Time						
Angle						
Area						

FIGURE 6 *INSET 5 year planning chart*

3   PLANNING IN THE CLASSROOM FOR THE CHILDREN'S LEARNING EXPERIENCES

Consider where the children are starting from. This will give the teacher support as he or she chooses the particular activities which will best deliver the aspect of measurement identified in the Year Group Plans. The teacher will need to take this information from a variety of sources, including school records, discussion with the children and/or possibly an assessment task. The teacher will then use this information to plan for the class.

Two models for this organisation are suggested here. The first is based on individual lines of development for each of the children in the class. The second is based on ability grouping. Both of these will require the teacher to list the possible activities from the Year Group plan that are available to deliver the particular aspect of measurement for the half term. The activities can then be grouped on a planning chart (see figure 7).

These activities are now in developmental order and represent a range of lines of development. There are three possible developments that children may be involved in from this starting point. The teacher may choose particular activities based on children's previous experiences, or based on their compatibility with the current class topic.

- The first is that they tackle several activities from the same section, and then the teacher decides that it is not appropriate for them to move on.
- The second is that they tackle one or two activities from each section and whizz through to the problems.
- The third is that, according to their response to the starting activity, the teacher moves them to the next section, or into the previous section.

4   PLANNING IN THE CLASSROOM FOR THE CHILDREN'S USE OF RESOURCES

- Each activity lists the resources that children will need. The teacher will need to ensure that the children can find these resources when they need them. Whenever possible, they should be allowed to select what they need for themselves.
- Many of the activities lend themselves to classroom display. This is identified in the text.

Aspect of measurement	Children's names	Learning objectives	Comments
(Taken from the year group plans) For example **Comparison** • Familiarity with the appropriate language: *longer than, shorter than the same as*, etc. • *Beads* • *Sorting box* • *Bodies* Date: Class:	**Model 1** *This lists the children who will start the programme of learning at these points.* **Model 2** *This identifies group names based on children's ability*	*This section contains a list of objectives that the teacher is hoping that the children will achieve by being involved with the activity.* *If this is to be used as an assessment activity, it may also identify particular evidence or benchmarks that the teacher may be looking for.*	*The completion of this section as the children are working allows the teacher to use this document as a means of recording what the children have achieved.*
Early experiences *For example* See *Beads* and Activities that some children might need to do first		*For example:* Can describe the relationship between three objects in terms of which is the longest, which is shortest and which is in the middle.	*For example:* Joseph described the relationship between all three: 'This one is longer than both of those'.
Teaching activities *For example* See *Beads* and Reinforcing activities that some children might need			
Extension activities *For example* See *Beads* and Activities that some children might be ready to move on to			
Problems See list of possible Problems at the beginning of the *Length* section			

FIGURE 7 *Chart for planning learning experiences in the classroom*

- The classroom organisation of each activity is identified in the text. It assumes that the children are sitting in groups, but that those groups may be actually working individually, in pairs or in larger groups.
- Much of the work assumes that the children have opportunities to discuss what they are doing, before, during and after the task. Again, this may be in pairs, in larger groups or as a class.

5   PLANNING IN THE CLASSROOM FOR A MEASUREMENT SESSION

Once the teacher has a clear idea about which activities the children need to experience, each session has to be planned. Teachers will need to plan for the following:

- **A balance of activities in the classroom**. Each activity offers an organisation structure in terms of teacher time, resources and space required. When the activities for each group of children for a particular session have been decided upon, the teacher needs to reflect on those plans. A structured lesson plan like the one in figure 8 may be useful. Checking each column will allow teachers to ensure that the plans are workable.

Activity	Children's names	Teacher time needed	Space needed	Resources needed
See *Beads*, Activities that some children might need to do first	Group 1	Two minutes' introduction then ten minutes' intervention after they have threaded the beads	Carpet area	Beads, paper

FIGURE 8 *Lesson plan*

- **How the session will be introduced.** From the planning sheet, will it be possible to introduce all the activities to all the children without expecting any of them to wait too long? If the children are beginning one of the problems, there will need to be a lot of discussion as they begin, and also an opportunity to 'take stock' along the way.

- **What will the children do when they finish?** From the planning sheet, is it likely that the groups will finish at different times? Are there activities planned for them when they do? Would one of the low teacher-intensive activities be useful at this point?
- **How will the activities finish?** Will the children have the opportunity to discuss the outcomes of what they have been doing, either as a class, as a group or with the teacher?

CHAPTER

THE ROLE OF THE TEACHER

As in most parts of the teacher's day, the role of the teacher in the teaching of measurement is wide and varied. In the text, there is an indication of how much teacher intervention will be required if the children are to get the most out of each activity. There are also suggestions for questions that the teacher may wish to ask to support the children's learning. In particular, the teacher will need to be prepared to be sensitive to a number of things as he or she does intervene:

- Many children (and adults too) find that one of the most difficult parts of any activity is the start. Actually getting your thoughts together is often the hardest thing to do. Teachers need to be prepared to help children over this hurdle by encouraging discussion with them and between them.

  > 'Where will you start?'
  > 'What do you know already?'
  > "What do you want to find out?'
  > 'What will you need?'

- Part of the process of learning is going down blind alleys. Teachers need to be aware that children actually need to follow an incorrect pathway as they work through a problem. They also need to be prepared to rescue children from those blind alleys when they need it.

  > 'Is this getting you anywhere?'
  > 'Would it be an idea to try something different?'
  > 'What is it you are trying to find out?'
  > 'What have some of the others done?'

- The most difficult thing for a teacher to do is not to intervene. There are many occasions when the children are better off without us, and are in a position of ownership with the problem that they are working on. Teachers need to seal their lips sometimes.

- Most children are not great at stopping to reflect on what they have done so far and staying focused on their target. Teachers need to encourage them to develop their skills by helping them to ask and answer questions like:

  'What did I know when I started?'
  'What do I know now?'
  'What am I trying to find out now?'
  'What will be the next step after that?'
  'How will I find that out?'
  'What will I need?'
  'Will I remember what I've done?'

Many of these points are close to being contradictory. Teachers will need to 'judge the moment' much of the time, and even consult the children: 'Shall I help you along here or are you doing better without me?' They are usually right!

SECTION B

MEASUREMENT ACTIVITIES

This section is divided into five chapters:

CHAPTER 4
Length

CHAPTER 5
Angle

CHAPTER 6
Mass

CHAPTER 7
Capacity/Volume

CHAPTER 8
Time

CHAPTER 4

LENGTH

This chapter includes:

- Introduction
- Beads
- Ten
- Sorting box
- How long?
- Plasticine sausages
- Bodies
- Detectives
- Make a line
- Metre mouse
- How high?
- Length activities for the rest of the class

The problems related to this section are:

- Make a giant ant, spider or bird to scale   (page 184)
- Make a model of the school   (page 184)
- Make a map of your classroom   (page 185)
- How much water will fill up the classroom?   (page 186)
- Make a box to carry 1 kilogram   (page 189)
- Parcels   (page 190)
- How many vital statistics can you find out about your body?   (page 191)
- Does your chair fit you?   (page 192)
- Make a trundle wheel   (page 192)
- How far away can you see a mouse?   (page 193)
- Make a bag to carry 5 kilograms   (page 194)
- Invent a new way of measuring   (page 194)
- Make a strip of paper 1 kilometre long   (page 195)
- Make a clock   (page 198)
- Make a hat   (page 198)
- How much space does your skin take up?   (page 199)
- How much wallpaper would you need to decorate the school?   (page 200)
- Ten metres of string   (page 200)
- Polyominoes   (page 201)

INTRODUCTION

There are a number of 'hidden' understandings that children may need to be helped with as they learn to measure in one dimension, which can be easily overlooked. They need to understand that:

- a specific length (width, etc.) has a start and end point. This is very apparent when children start to compare two objects and they neglect to compare them from the same base line;
- 'distance' is the space between two points or objects, whether or not a line has been drawn between them;
- circumference and perimeter can be represented by length. It must be extremely confusing for children that a boundary around a two-dimensional space is measured as a one-dimensional line;
- length, width, height, depth, distance, circumference are all words which indicate a measurement or comparison of lengths;
- lengths (widths and so on) can be compared and ordered.

The National Curriculum suggests certain goals at each Key Stage in the understanding of linear measure (see figure 9).

	Pupils should be taught to:
Key Stage 1	**a** compare objects and events using the appropriate language, by direct comparison and then standard units of length, begin to use a wider range of standard units; choosing units appropriate to the situation; estimate with these units **b** choose and use simple measuring instruments, reading and interpreting numbers and scales with some accuracy
Key Stage 2	**a** choose appropriate standard units of length and make sensible estimates with them in everyday situations; extend their understanding of the relationships between units; convert one metric unit to another; know the rough metric equivalents of imperial units still in daily use **b** choose and use appropriate measuring instruments; interpret numbers and read scales to an increasing degree of accuracy **c** find perimeters of simple shapes; find practically the circumference of circles, being introduced to the ratio π

FIGURE 9 *Key Stage goals – Length*

ACTIVITY 1   BEADS

```
─────────────── LEARNING OBJECTIVES ───────────────
1    Comparing objects using appropriate language by direct
     comparison and then using common non-standard units
     of length.
2    Understanding comparatives.
```

What you will need

The children will need some beads to thread. They will need to be
all the same size. If beads are not available, interlocking cubes or
cotton reels can be used.

What to do

Ask the children to co-operate to make a chain with all the beads in
the container. When it is finished, let them:

- hold one end and wiggle it;
- drop a hoop on the snake (either on a wiggle or on a straight
  part);
- estimate how many beads are inside and how many are outside
  the hoop.

Ask questions:

- Where should you drop the hoop to get the most beads inside?
- Where should you drop the hoop to get the most beads
  outside?
- How many different answers are possible to this problem?
- How will you record your results?
  (Some children will choose to draw pictures, others may write
  sums, others may choose to use a combination of the two.)
- How will you know you have all the results?

Organisation

Actually making the 'snake' is an interesting social exercise and is
best suited for a group of three or four. The most difficult thing for
a teacher to do is not to intervene. It is interesting to reflect on the
system they developed afterwards, and whether or not they think it
was a good one.

The wiggling of the snake causes much excitement, and really needs to be introduced to the whole class, because they will all want to watch. A discussion on counting methods will be useful to the children.

- Is there a way to count quickly?
- Can the snake be marked or organised in any way to make the counting easier?

Once they have been introduced to the idea, small groups of children can be left to make up their own 'sums'. If the children record their sums in a colourful way, they can be used to make an attractive display.

Activities that some children might need to do first

1 Using only seven beads, let the children take it in turns to:
- step on the threaded beads;
- let their partner guess how many beads are 'hiding';
- check to see if they were right.

It is interesting to watch how some children will make 'wild' guesses, and others will try to calculate how many beads are hidden. (SSM4a)

2 Ask the children to:
- make a chain with thirty or more beads;
- sit on part of it;
- find out how many beads are peeping and how many are sat on.

Reinforcing activities that some children might need

1 Use more or fewer beads in the chain.

2 Let the children step on the middle of a chain.
- How many beads peep out at the left?
- How many beads peep out at the right?
- How many beads are stepped on?

This idea can be developed in the same way as the earlier activity, by making it a game, and then setting a challenge to find all combinations. (SSM4a)

3 *Ten.*

Activities that some children might be ready to move on to

1 Make a chain with all the beads in the container. How many people do you need to cover it up:
- with their feet?
- with their legs and bottoms?
- with their bodies?
- with their bodies and arms?

The children will need to develop and use careful methods of counting the beads in this activity. They may choose to:
- join the beads so that they are in sets of five or ten of a single colour, so that they are easier to count;
- join the beads in sets of two so they are easier to count;
- mark the chain with a tag, every time they get to five or ten.

2   *Metre mouse.*

3   *Detectives.*

Similar activities for other measures

AREA
- *Body prints*
- *Body measures*
- *Cotton wool balls*
- *Shadows*
- *Boxes*
- *Letter shapes*

CAPACITY/VOLUME
- *Paint*
- *Fill a pot*
- *Sinkers*

WEIGHT
- *Envelopes*

ACTIVITY 2   # TEN

┌─────────────── LEARNING OBJECTIVES ───────────────┐
│ 1   Comparing objects using appropriate language by direct comparison. │
│ 2   Using common non-standard units of length and estimating with those units. │
│ 3   Developing different mathematical approaches and looking for ways to overcome difficulties. │
└──┘

What you will need
The children will need:

- some collections of small objects, e.g. crayons, chalk, pens, paper clips, toothpicks, lolly sticks, etc.;
- some oddments of wallpaper.

What to do

On a large sheet of paper (wallpaper is best), children take it in turns to:

- choose a unit of measure;
- estimate how far they think ten will reach if placed end to end;
- place ten on the paper to check.

The children will need to agree on a scoring system, and how close the estimates have to be to warrant a score. What they decide is not really important, but the process of discussion and agreement is an interesting one!

Organisation

This game needs to be played by a group, but several groups can be playing at the same time. The teacher can spend time with each of the groups and discuss the outcomes.

Once the game has been introduced in this way, groups of three or four children can play on their own with little supervision, while the rest of the class are engaged in a more teacher-intensive activity.

Activities that some children might need to do first

1 *Detectives.*

2 *Make a line.*

3 *Beads.*

4 *Sorting box.*

Reinforcing activities that some children might need

1 *Bodies.*

2 Play the same game, but roll a die or spin a spinner to find out how many units long the line needs to be. (SSM4a)

3 *How long?*

4 *Plasticine sausages.*

Activities that some children might be ready to move on to

1 Extend the activity above by using ten of any object to make a ruler with, and use it to measure. Try using twenty or thirty to make a ruler. (SSM4a)

2 *Metre mouse.*

3 *How high?*

Similar activities for other measures

AREA
- *Body prints*
- *Body measures*
- *Cotton wool balls*
- *Shadows*
- *Boxes*
- *Letter shapes*

CAPACITY/VOLUME
- *Paint*
- *Fill a pot*
- *Sinkers*

MASS
- *Envelopes*

ACTIVITY 3   SORTING BOX

LEARNING OBJECTIVES
---

1   Comparing objects using appropriate language by direct comparison and then using common non-standard units of length.
2   Understanding the language of comparatives.

What you will need

The children will need a 'sorting box' for these activities.

The box will contain a collection of objects, for example: toys, cards, boxes, ribbons, string, sticks, bottles and tins of different heights, building blocks.

What to do

Put a variety of things from the sorting box into a bag. Begin the session by playing a game with the children. Ask them to close their eyes and choose two objects from the bag. Ask them to compare the objects *without looking*, using language like:

- 'This one is longer than that one';
- 'They are both the same length';
- 'This one is the shortest'.

If they are correct, they can keep the objects. If not, they go back in the bag. The child who has the most things from the sorting box when the bag is empty wins the game. (This game can also be played with eyes open!)

Follow up the game by setting specific tasks, e.g. give the children an object, such as a paintbrush, and ask them to find something longer and something shorter. They can record their findings by drawing what they have found to show which is the longest, shortest, etc. Discuss their records. Can their friends tell from the drawings which objects are the longest?

Organisation

The game can be introduced to the whole class or to a group. The teacher will need to be a part of the group to encourage discussion, but the children can then be left to find and record objects on their own. It is likely that the children will enjoy the game, and will choose to play it on their own (after a fashion!), unsupervised.

If the teacher is working with the group, the rest of the class will need to be engaged in one of the activities at the end of the section.

Activities that some children might need to do first

1   Have a scavenger hunt. Choose something in the room, e.g. a paintbrush, and ask the children to bring something from home which is:
   • a bit longer;
   • much longer;
   • about the same;
   • a bit shorter;
   • a lot shorter.
   Discuss how they will remember the length.
   Discuss how useful a standard measure might be. (SSM4a)

2   *Plasticine sausages.*

3   *Beads.*

Reinforcing activities that some children might need

1   Play *'Who am I?'*. With some friends, agree on a unit of measure, e.g. centimetres, decimetres, paper clips. Children take it in turns to be blindfolded. The other children choose something from the sorting box, measure it and replace it. The blindfolded child is told the length and then has to guess what the object is. For example, the clue might be: 'I measure thirteen paperclips long'. Children get three tries to find the right object. If they find it, they keep it, and the object is replaced by something new from the sorting box. (SSM4a)

2   *How long?*

Activities that some children might be ready to move on to

1   You need a pile of about ten interesting objects from the sorting box which are all of
     different lengths. Two children take it in turns to hide their eyes. The other child chooses
     one object and measures it to the nearest centimetre. They then replace the object and
     tell their opponent the length. The first child must open their eyes and try to find the
     object as soon as possible. (SSM4a)

2   *Bodies.*

3   *Make a line.*

Similar activities for other measures

AREA
- *Shadows*
- *Boxes*
- *Letter shapes*

CAPACITY/VOLUME
- The children will need a 'sorting box' for this activity, containing a collection of
  containers which will hold different amounts.
      Put a variety of containers from the sorting box into a box. Ask the children to choose
  two objects and order them, using language like: 'This one holds more than that one' or
  'They will both hold the same' or 'This one will hold the least'.
      If they are correct, they can keep the containers. If not, they go back in the box. The
  child who has the most things from the sorting box when the box is empty, wins the game.
  (SSM4a)

- *Cones*

MASS
- The children will need a 'sorting box' for this activity, containing a collection of objects of
  different weights, for example: toys, boxes, keys, a feather, a few vegetables, building blocks.
      Put a variety of things from the sorting box into a bag. Ask the children to choose two
  objects and order them, using language like: 'This one is heavier than that one' or 'They
  are both the same weight' or 'This one is the lightest'.
      If they are correct, they can keep the objects. If not, they go back in the bag. The child
  who has the most things from the sorting box when the bag is empty wins the game.
      Follow up the game by setting specific tasks, e.g. give the children an object, such as a
  lump of plasticine and ask them to find something heavier and something lighter. They
  can record their findings by drawing what they have found to show which is the heaviest,
  lightest, etc. Discuss their records. Can their friends tell from the drawings which objects
  are the heaviest? (SSM4a)

  - *Plasticine models*
  - *Magnets*

TIME
- *Take your time*
- *Modelling*

ACTIVITY **4**   # HOW LONG?

┌─────────────── LEARNING OBJECTIVES ───────────────┐

1   Comparing objects using appropriate language by direct comparison.
2   Using common non-standard units of length and estimating with those units.
3   Discussing work, responding to and asking mathematical questions.

└──┘

What you will need

The children will need:
- string or ribbon;
- a collection of junk boxes of different sizes;
- sticky labels.

What to do

Ask the children to cut lengths of string or ribbon to measure the girths of some boxes, and label them either with words or, better still, with numbers. They will need to indicate which dimension is being measured. (Remember the strings need labelling too!)

Ask them to order the boxes in the order they think their girths will fall. Then order the ribbons and compare. Discuss the measurements with them:

- Which was the fattest? Thinnest?
- Which ones were easy to guess?
- Which ones were more difficult?
- What do you think it was that made them difficult?
- What do you think we would find if we measured round them longways?

Teachers may feel that it is appropriate for the children to take these new measurements and make comparisons.

Organisation

This activity works best as a group activity because the boxes take up a lot of space, and lots of boxes would be needed for the whole class to work on the activity together. However, once they understand the task, the children can get on and measure and label them with little input from the teacher. They will need some direction with the discussion.

Alternatively, teachers may prefer to let two groups of children prepare the boxes and ribbons for the other group. This can turn the activity into a game, with children taking it in turns to try to match boxes and ribbons. If they are correct, they keep the ribbon: if not, they replace it.

Children who are not involved in the activity will need to be involved in another activity which allows the teacher to escape for a short time when the children have finished labelling.

Activities that some children might need to do first

1 How far do you think a ball of wool will reach? Guess and check. Try string, elastic bands, etc. (SSM4a)

2 *Beads.*

3 *Sorting box.*

Reinforcing activities that some children might need

1 Use a collection of round objects (tins, balls, fruit, etc.). Let the children cut a piece of string, paper or ribbon to the length they think they will need to fit round exactly. Stick them on to check. (SSM4a)

2 *Plasticine sausages.*

Activities that some children might be ready to move on to

1 Use a collection of round things, e.g. tins, balls, fruit, etc. Find the diameters and perimeters of some. Is there a relationship between the diameter and the perimeter? (SSM4a,c)

2 *Bodies.*

3 *Detectives.*

Similar activities for other measures

AREA	TIME	WEIGHT	CAPACITY/VOLUME
• *Shadows*	• *Take your time*	• *Plasticine models*	• *Cones*
• *Boxes*	• *Modelling*	• *Magnets*	• *Paint*
• *Letter shapes*			

ACTIVITY 5   PLASTICINE SAUSAGES

┌─────────────── LEARNING OBJECTIVES ───────────────┐

1   Comparing objects using appropriate language by direct
    comparison.
2   Using common non-standard units of length and
    estimating with those units.
3   Understanding the language of comparatives.

└──┘

What you will need

The children will need some plasticine and somewhere to roll it
out.

What to do

Ask the children to roll out a plasticine sausage until they think it is
long enough for a bracelet for themselves.

Let them try it on to see how close the guess is, and then change
it if necessary.

Discuss the children's attempts with them.

- Was your bracelet too long? Too short?
- Was your bracelet strong enough?
- How could you make it stronger?

Encourage the children to use the correct language: 'too long', 'too
short', 'a little bit too long', etc. Ask them to make another sausage
to make a necklace, or an ankle bracelet or a belt. Leave them to
make some jewellery for a friend, or their teacher.

Organisation

Because of the importance of the discussion, this activity needs
input from the teacher. Consequently, it needs to be a group activity
for about six children.

The rest of the class can be involved in making plasticine
sausages, and using them to make the letters of their name, for
example, or one of the activities at the end of the section, or
some other activity which requires little attention from the
teacher.

Activities that some children might need to do first

1 Let the children roll out a plasticine snake and then:
   • find something straight which is longer;
   • find something curved which is longer;
   • find something straight which is shorter;
   • find something curved which is shorter;
   • find something straight which is the same length;
   • find something curved which is the same length;
   • find something straight which is twice as long;
   • find something curved which is twice as long.
   (SSM4a)

2 Five children each make a plasticine sausage and use them to play the sentence game.
   They take it in turns to make up a new sentence about the snakes, e.g. 'Gemma's snake is
   longer than Toni's'. If they successfully invent a new sentence, they collect a cube. The
   player with the most cubes after four (five or six) rounds is the winner.
      (The game can be extended to using word cards so the children make up written
   sentences. Words are offered on the worksheet on page 40.) Alternatively, ask a group of
   children to make up sentences about each other, or a set of different length ribbons, or
   classroom objects. (SSM4a)

3 *Sorting box.*

Reinforcing activities that some children might need

1 Play a game using plasticine. Use a set of cards with curved or straight lines on. Without
   testing, children roll out a snake which they think is the same length. If they are right,
   they keep the card. The first player with five cards wins the game.
      This game can be extended to using a set of number cards; children take it in turns to
   take a card, and try to roll out their plasticine into a snake which is the appropriate
   number of centimetres in length. They can also use a dice or spinner to generate the
   numbers. (SSM4a)

2 *Detectives.*

3 *Bodies.*

Activities that some children might be ready to move on to

1 Let the children roll out a plasticine sausage until they think it is long enough for five
   teddy bear counters or cubes to stand along it exactly. Try it to see how close the guess is.
   Change it if necessary.
      Discuss the children's attempts with them. Encourage them to use the correct language:
   'too long', 'too short', 'a little bit too long', etc. Try also five crayons, five toy cars, and
   other numbers.
      Extend to asking how much plasticine is needed to make a sausage for five children to
   stand along? Lie along? (SSM4a)

2   Ask the children to use plasticine sausages to make shapes.
Roll three pieces of plasticine into sausages, and make a triangle. Can you always make a triangle? Is there a rule for when you can and when you cannot? Explore different triangles and other shapes. (SSM4a)

3   *How long?*

Similar activities for other measures

AREA	TIME	MASS	CAPACITY/VOLUME
• *Shadows*	• *How long*	• *Plasticine models*	• *Cones*
• *Boxes*	• *Plasticine models*	• *Magnets*	
• *Letter shapes*			

ACTIVITY 6   BODIES

> ── LEARNING OBJECTIVES ──
>
> 1   Comparing objects using appropriate language by direct comparison.
> 2   Using common non-standard units of length and estimating with those units.
> 3   Using a variety of forms of mathematical representation.

What you will need

The children will need:

- string;
- scissors;
- large sheets of sugar paper;
- sticky labels.

What to do

1   Let the children make an outline of their hands with string (rather like drawing round!) (see figure 10). It is a good idea to use sticky labels to name them. Ask them whose string they predict to be the longest.

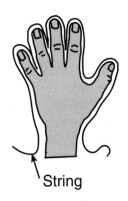
String

FIGURE 10 *Hand outline*

Stretch them out and compare outlines. Let the children make them into a graph by sticking them onto paper. Discuss the outcomes.
- Who had the longest/shortest outline?
- Were they all similar?
- Were there any surprises? Did you expect this to happen?
- Why are they not all the same?

2 Let the children work in pairs to collect data for and respond to the following challenges:
- Can the person with the largest outline also hold the most number of cubes? Does it make a difference how you hold them?
- Does the graph to show who has the longest fingers put people in the same order?
- Does the graph to show who has the longest foot outline put people in the same order?
- Is hand outline related to height?
- Is hand outline related to age?

It may be appropriate for each group of children to investigate one of these questions using a computer database to record and represent their findings.

Organisation

In this activity, the teacher needs to set the children going and to spend some time discussing the outcomes of the first part of the activity with them. There also needs to be some discussion about how the children plan to attempt the second part of the activity.

- How will they collect their information?
- What information do they need?
- Who will collect it?
- How will they represent it?
- How will it help them find out the solution to their challenge?

After that, apart from 'passing by' occasionally, the teacher can usually leave the children to work independently on their task.

Teachers may choose to offer the activity to a group, half the class, or the whole class. Each of these would be appropriate, provided the rest of the class are usefully occupied, either with one of the activities at the end of the section, or some other activity which at first does not require the teacher's attention.

Activities that some children might need to do first

1   Make 'physical graphs' with the children. Ask them to line up in order of height, total finger length, arm length, leg length, etc. Measurements may be comparative, non-standard or standard.

Let the children find a way of recording their findings, e.g. making models, using straws to represent length, using plasticine sausages to represent length. (SSM4a)

2   *How long?*

3   *Sorting box.*

Reinforcing activities that some children might need

1   Measure the circumference of your ankle with string. Compare it with the circumference of your fist and the length of your foot. Look at other people's results. Discuss whether there is a relationship between some of the measurements, e.g. Do two fists make a forearm?

Extend or develop by asking the question, 'Could you buy yourself some socks if you could only use your fist as a measure? (SSM4a,c)

2   Similarly, is there a relationship between upper arm length and height? Develop this into historical problems, e.g. a caveman's bones have been found; can you find out his height? (SSM4a)

3   *Make a line.*

Activities that some children might be ready to move on to

1   Ask the children to find out who is long legged, short legged and average legged. Measure how tall people are standing, sitting and kneeling. Extend the idea to opening a clothes factory - how many of each size, (small, medium and large) would you make? Which sized people would each size hope to fit? (SSM4a)

2   Let each child in a group measure, record and order the length of an agreed set of body parts, e.g. head circumference, head size (height and width), waist, wrist, height, reach. Let them record their findings with string or strips of paper. Use them for the following:
   • Put your own body parts in order.
   • Predict and test any ratios, e.g. how many heads to a height?
   • Do you have a long thin face, or a short fat one?
   • Use the strips to make scale graphs, e.g. fold each piece of paper in half, or quarters and make a graph of the group's results for height. (SSM4a,c)

3   *Detectives.*

Similar activities for other measures

AREA	WEIGHT	TIME
• *Shadows*	• *Plasticine models*	• *How long?*
• *Boxes*	• *Magnets*	
• *Letter shapes*		

ACTIVITY 7 DETECTIVES

── LEARNING OBJECTIVES ──

1 Comparing objects using appropriate language by direct comparison.
2 Using common non-standard units of length.
3 Understanding comparatives.

What you will need

The children will need a set of 'clue cards' made from the worksheet on page 41.

What to do

The teacher needs to identify one object in the room which fits each description before the session begins. Let the children be 'detectives' and use the clue cards to find objects that fit the description.

Teachers may feel that it is appropriate to ask the children to make a written or pictorial record of the 'suspects', before they reveal the culprit (i.e. the objects chosen earlier).

Organisation

This activity works best for a group because of the moving around involved. Provided the children can read the clues, they require little of the teacher's attention, once their role as detective is made clear.

The teacher may feel able to work with another group on an activity which demands a little more of his or her attention, while the rest of the class can be involved in one of the activities at the end of the section.

Activities that some children might need to do first

1 *How long?*

2 *Plasticine sausages.*

3 *Sorting box.*

Reinforcing activities that some children might need

1   Have a collecting race. Give the children three categories:
  • longer than your foot;
  • shorter than your leg;
  • nearly the same length as your arm.
  Who can find the most objects for each list in five minutes? (SSM4a)

2   *Make a line.*

3   *Bodies.*

Activities that some children might be ready to move on to

1   Have a collecting race. Give the children three categories:
  • between 1 cm and 5 cm;
  • between 10 cm and 15 cm;
  • between 20 cm and 25 cm.
  Who can find the most objects for each list in five minutes? (SSM4a,b)

2   Let the children make length puzzles for other children to solve.
  • I am between 10 cm and 25 cm tall.
  • I am 15 cm round.
  • My top is about 9 cm across.
  This can be made easier by adding other clues, e.g. colour. (SSM4a,b)

3   *How high?*

Similar activities for other measures

AREA
  • *Shadows*
  • *Boxes*
  • *Letter shapes*

TIME
  • *How long?*

WEIGHT
  • Make a set of clue cards similar to those in Figure 12, about weight. The teacher needs to identify one object in the room which fits each description. Let the children be 'detectives' and use the clue cards to find objects that fit the description.
    Teachers may feel that it is appropriate to ask the children to make a written or pictorial record of the 'suspects', before they reveal the culprit (i.e. the objects chosen earlier). (SSM4a)
  • *Plasticine models*
  • *Magnets*

CAPACITY/VOLUME
- The children will need a collection of containers which hold a variety of amounts, and will need to make a set of clue cards which relate to that set of containers. Let the children be 'detectives' and use the clue cards to find the containers which fit the descriptions.

  Teachers may feel that it is appropriate to ask the children to make a written or pictorial record of the 'suspects', before they reveal the culprit (i.e. the containers chosen earlier). (SSM4a)

ACTIVITY 8   MAKE A LINE

┌─────────────── LEARNING OBJECTIVES ───────────────┐
│   │
│ 1   Comparing objects using appropriate language by direct │
│   comparison.   │
│ 2   Using common non-standard units of length.   │
│ 3   Developing different mathematical approaches and │
│   looking for ways to overcome difficulties.   │
│   │
└──┘

What you will need

The children will need a collection of empty boxes of different sizes and something to draw with.

What to do

The children need a chalk line each, drawn on the floor, at least one and a half metres long. They take it in turns to choose a box and place it on their line, or to swap one of their boxes for one of a different size. The first player to cover their line exactly wins the game.

Alternatively:

- the lines need not be straight;
- the lines need not be the same length;
- the boxes could all be the same size;
- the children could play with shorter lines and smaller boxes on their desks;
- the children could draw each others' lines.

Organisation

This activity works well for a group of between three and five children, so that they do not have to wait too long for their turn.

Teachers will need to work with them for the first and maybe the second game, but then most children will be able to work through a game on their own. If the first group has been carefully chosen, one of the children can often be used to teach other children how to play.

Ask the children to record their game by drawing the line, and sticking the boxes on a long piece of paper or onto the wall with masking tape.

The rest of the class can either try one of the activities at the end of the section, or be engaged in another reasonably independent task.

Activities that some children might need to do first

1 Order boxes according to their size.

2 *How long?*

3 *Sorting box.*

Reinforcing activities that some children might need

1 Ask the children to take six boxes. (Giant boxes to use on the floor or smaller ones on the desk.) Set them one of the following challenges:
   • Make the longest line you can with the boxes.
   • Make the shortest line you can with the boxes.
   • How many different lines can you make with the boxes?
   • Order the boxes in three ways (height, width, depth); discuss the differences in each sort.
   • Undo the boxes - what is the longest line you can make now? (SSM4a)

2 *Bodies.*

3 *Detectives.*

Activities that some children might be ready to move on to

1 Use glue or tape and ask the children to choose their own boxes:
   • What is the tallest tower you can build with six boxes?
   • What is the shortest tower you can build with six boxes?
   • Can you build a tower exactly the same height as one of the children in the group with six boxes?
   • Can you build a tower as tall as your teacher with six boxes? (SSM4a)

2 *How high?*

3 *Metre mouse.*

Similar activities for other measures

AREA

- Play a similar game, but ask the children to cover a surface with their boxes; for example, use a sheet of A4 for small boxes on the desk, or a sheet of newspaper if they are playing with larger boxes on the floor. The surfaces to be covered need not be all the same size, provided the rule is clear, that the surface must be covered as completely as possible.
    Set similar challenges:
  1 Cover the greatest surface you can with the boxes. (The children will need to develop a means of checking this. Their discussion sometimes leads them to using a standard unit, i.e. a standard box.)
  2 Make the shortest line you can with the boxes.
  3 How many different surfaces can you make with the boxes?
  4 Can you use the boxes to make a rectangular shape?
  5 Can you cover your desk (or chair or teacher's table) with any six boxes?
  6 Undo the boxes - what is the largest area you can cover now? (SSM4a,c)
- *Shadows*
- *Boxes*
- *Letter shapes*

TIME

- *How long?*

WEIGHT

- *Plasticine models*
- *Magnets*

CAPACITY/VOLUME

- Play a similar game, but ask the children to fill a large box with their boxes. They could use a large cereal box if they were playing on the desk, or a large cardboard carton if they are playing with larger boxes on the floor. The boxes to be filled need not be all the same size, provided the rule is clear, that the box must be filled as completely as possible.
    Set challenges:
  1 Fill the largest space you can using any six boxes. (The children will need to be encouraged to discuss a standard way of testing this. It is very difficult, and the most usual outcome at KS1 is to test by eye! At KS2 the children can be expected to think of other methods.)
  2 Fill the smallest space you can with six boxes.
  3 Can you use some boxes to make a cuboid? Cube? Staircase?
  4 Can you cover your desk (or chair or teacher's table) with any six boxes?
  5 Order six boxes according to how many play bricks (for example) they can hold.
  6 Undo the six boxes - which covers the largest area? Did the box which covers the largest area also hold the most bricks? (SSM4a,c)

ACTIVITY 9 # METRE MOUSE

─── LEARNING OBJECTIVES ───

1   Choosing appropriate standard units of length.
2   Extending understanding of the relationship between units.
3   Interpreting numbers and reading scales to an increasing
    degree of accuracy.
4   Selecting and using the appropriate mathematics and
    materials.

What you will need

The children will need:

- a metre stick for each pair;
- a 0-10 spinner or two dice;
- a mouse for each player (see page 42) or a centimetre cube;
- a piece of cheese (or yellow plasticine!) for each player.

What to do

Ask a pair of children to play *Metre mouse*. They need to put the
cheese at the end of the ruler. Each child chooses one side of the
ruler, and puts their mouse at the start of their side.

Players take it in turn to roll the dice or spin the spinner and
move their 'mouse' that many centimetres along the ruler. The first
mouse to the cheese wins the game.

Organisation

Most children find this to be a relatively straightforward game.
Once they understand the rules, they can usually be left to play one
or two games without supervision.

Teachers may find it appropriate to teach the game to the whole
class (the class against the teacher!) as a demonstration, and then
use it as a game that children can turn to in a quiet moment.

Activities that some children might need to do first

1   Use a metre of string, paper or card. Use it to make patterns and pictures. Provide a set of
    task cards. (SSM4a)

2   *Ten.*

3   *Beads.*

Reinforcing activities that some children might need

1   Use a metre of string and cut it into four unequal lengths. Stick them on card in order. Measure each one and add the lengths. (SSM4a)

2   *Bodies.*

3   *Make a line.*

Activities that some children might be ready to move on to

1   Let the children make a metre strip from a sheet of A4, either centimetre squared paper or plain paper. (SSM4a)

2   *How high?*

Similar activities for other measures

AREA
- *Grids*
- *Make a square metre*

CAPACITY/VOLUME
- *Sponges*
- *Blanket box*
- *Elastic bands*
- *Fill a litre*
- *200 grams of plasticine*
- *Guess which box*

MASS
- *Weigh yourself*
- *Gravel balance*
- *Popcorn*
- *How many stones?*

ACTIVITY 10 HOW HIGH?

LEARNING OBJECTIVES
---

1   Choosing appropriate standard units of length and making sensible estimates with them in everyday situations.

2   Extending understanding of the relationship between units; converting one metric unit to another; choosing and using appropriate measuring instruments.

3   Interpreting numbers and scales with an increasing level of accuracy.

4   Presenting information and results clearly and explaining the reasons for the choice of presentation.

What you will need

The children will need large or long pieces of paper to record their findings, e.g. old till rolls.

What to do

Ask the children to find out how high or how far they can reach when they are jumping, hopping, standing on tiptoe, kneeling, standing, etc! Can the same people always reach the highest or the furthest?

Ask them to find ways to illustrate the information. They may decide that it is not necessary to use standard measures for their recording and that it is adequate to make comparisons and, for example, give each person a score according to where they rank in the group. They may suggest: database, pictures, graphs; discuss with the children the most appropriate method of display, to enable them to answer their questions.

Organisation

Because of the 'leaping around' involved, this activity works best if a small group at a time are testing themselves. All the information for the whole class can be collected and recorded on a chart over a few days. Alternatively, the teacher may choose to use an allotted hall time so that the whole class can collect their information at the same time. The whole class can then be involved in the discussion about how best to represent the information and whether it would be useful for different children in the class to represent it in different ways for comparison. This is a useful discussion and gives the children a chance to develop opinions about the advantages and disadvantages of different forms of representation.

The information itself does not take long to collect, so provided the children can be excused - a group at a time - they can be occupied in any other activity.

Activities that some children might need to do first

1   Build towers with anything: tins, bricks, blocks, boxes. Which can you build to the same height, or taller than you? (SSM4a)

2   *Beads.*

3   *Plasticine sausages.*

Reinforcing activities that some children might need

1   Use body parts as arbitrary measures. Fit children along a rope, a washing line, the edge of the playground, the classroom wall, etc. Let them sit, stand, lie, use their arm, finger, span, reach, step. Let them choose which is the most appropriate measure.

Provide workcards with tasks - some where the children are invited to use a particular part of their body to measure with.

For example:

- use handspans to measure the play house;
- use a part of your body to measure the playground. (SSM4a)

2   *Make a line.*

Activities that some children might be ready to move on to

1   Let the children make models of horses (either 2D or 3D) using horse hands as a unit of measure. Let three groups make a model with the 'same' height using a child's hands, a woman's hands, a man's hands. Discuss their findings. Discuss standard measure. (SSM4a)

2   *Metre mouse.*

Similar activities for other measures

CAPACITY/VOLUME

- *Guess which box*

LENGTH ACTIVITIES FOR THE REST OF THE CLASS

These ideas are designed for children to use with little support from the teacher, other than initial clarification. Teachers may choose to turn them into worksheets or challenge cards, or simply to explain to the children what is expected of them. Some activities are appropriate for a group to work on, others can be used with a whole class.

1   Play Hickory Dickory Dock. Use:
- centicubes or Cuisenaire 'ones';
- pictures of mice which are 10 cm long (see worksheet on page 42);
- a picture of a grandfather clock which is a metre tall.

Children take it in turns to roll a dice and take the appropriate number of cubes. When anyone has ten, they can be exchanged for a 10 cm mouse. When ten mice are collected, they can climb up the clock. (SSM4a)

2 Use a metre of string, paper or ribbon. Cut it up. Use the pieces to make patterns and pictures. Stick them on to card. (SSM4a)

3 Measure, record and order the length of ten of your body parts, for example:
- head circumference;
- head size;
- waist;
- wrist;
- height;
- reach; etc.

(SSM4c)

4 Make a race track on the floor or on a big table. Take it in turns to:
- roll a die;
- count hand or foot lengths along the race track (children may prefer to make a cut-out version of their own hand... or several).

The first person to the end wins. (SSM4a)

5 Make ten different snakes (e.g. plasticine). Sort the snakes onto a tree diagram, using labels such as 'longer than/not longer than', 'shorter than/not shorter than'.
Choose and use other objects, e.g. crayon, paintbrush. (Use the worksheet on page 43 where the snakes crawl along the path to the right hole.) (SSM4a)

6 Order a collection of straws or ribbons of different lengths according to their length. (SSM4a)

7 How many different measurements can you find on your body? Measure and record your own. (SSM4a)

8 How many different circumferences can you find on your body? Measure and record your own. (SSM4a,c)

9 Find five or six balls. Use string or linked paperclips to find the circumference of each. Record it. (SSM4a)

10 Use five strips of paper the same length. Use them to make a paper chain. Use it to measure with.
- Find five things longer.
- Find five things shorter and the same.
- Find five things about the same. (SSM4a)

is longer than

is shorter than

are longer than

are the same as

are shorter than

is the same as

FIGURE 11   *Worksheet 7* – Plasticine sausages
Hodder & Stoughton © 1996 Janine Blinko and Ann Slater Teaching Measures. The publishers grant permission for multiple copies of this worksheet to be made in the place of purchase for use solely in that institution.

FIGURE 12 *Worksheet 8* – Detectives

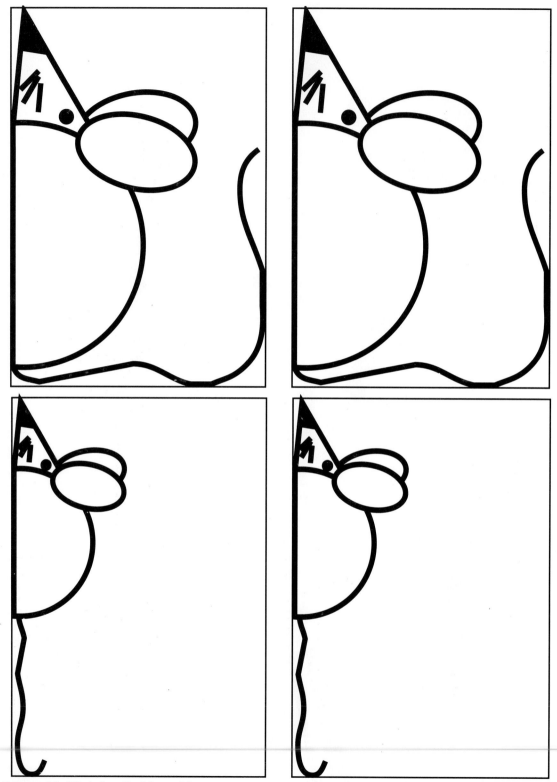

FIGURE 13   *Worksheet 9* – Metre Mouse

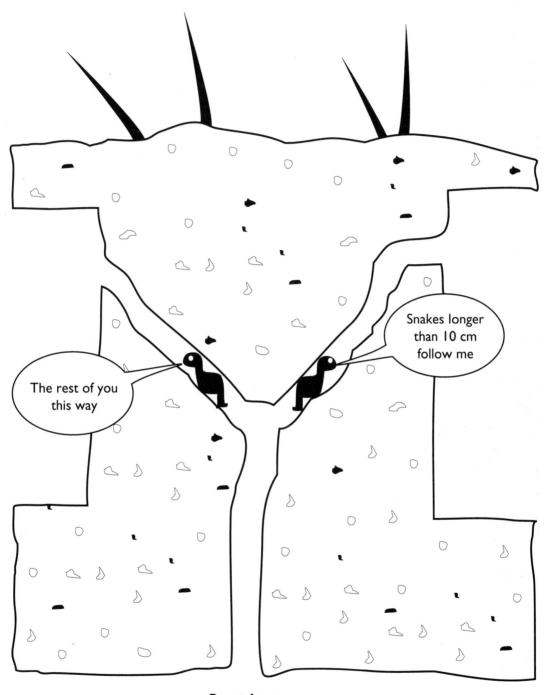

Start here

FIGURE 14 *Worksheet 10 –* Length activities for the rest of the class
Hodder & Stoughton © 1996 Janine Blinko and Ann Slater Teaching Measures. The publishers grant permission for multiple copies of this worksheet to be made in the place of purchase for use solely in that institution.

CHAPTER ANGLE

This chapter includes:

- Introduction
- Flowers
- Towers
- Turn!
- Letters
- Make two circles
- Doors
- Angle activities for the rest of the class

The problems related to this section are:

- Make a model of the school   (page 184)
- Make a map of your classroom   (page 185)
- Invent a new way of measuring   (page 194)
- Make a hat   (page 198)

INTRODUCTION

The perception of angle has always been one of a static block of space. Many children, when asked what an angle is, will respond that it is the space between two lines. The notion that angle is a measurement of turn has its own difficulties with which children will need support. They need to understand that:

- a turn has a start and an end;
- no matter how long or short the lines at the boundaries of the angle are, the angle remains constant;
- anything can turn right or left, clockwise or anticlockwise, and angle is the measurement of that turn.

The National Curriculum suggests certain goals at each Key Stage in the understanding of measurement (see figure 15).

	Pupils should be taught to:
Key Stage 1	**a** describe positions, using common words; recognise movements in a straight line, i.e. translation, and rotations, and combine them in simple ways; copy, continue and make patterns
	b understand angle as a measure of turn and recognise quarter turns and half turns, e.g. giving instructions for a rotating programmable toy; recognise right angles
Key Stage 2	**a** transform 2D shapes by rotation and visualise movements
	c use right angles, fractions of a turn and, later, degrees to measure rotation, and use the associated language

FIGURE 15 *Key Stage goals – Angle*

ACTIVITY 1   FLOWERS

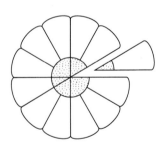

FIGURE 16 *A completed flower*

——— LEARNING OBJECTIVES ———

1 Understanding angle as a measurement of turn and recognising quarter turns and half turns.
2 Organising and checking work.

What you will need

The children will need some game pieces and game boards made from card (copied from the worksheet on page 56).

What to do

The children take it in turns to choose a petal and place it on the table. The aim is to complete a flower by placing the last petal in a flower. A player who places the last petal in any flower scores a point.

Once all the flowers are full, the game ends and players count up their scores.

Organisation

Teachers may choose to introduce this game in one of three ways:

•   to a group of children, where the group plays against the teacher. Once they understand the game, a pair of children can play on their own. The rest of the class will need to be engaged in one of the activities at the end of this section, or some other activity which requires little of the teacher's attention;

- to two children on their own. Those children should then be expected to teach others;
- to the whole class who have sorted themselves into groups, each group having two teams of two or three. There will need to be one set of the game for each group. The teacher will be very busy for this session!

Once the children understand the game, they can play on their own.

Activities that some children might need to do first

1   Jigsaw puzzles. (SSM2a)

2   Make mosaic-type patterns with commercially produced shape equipment. (SSM2a)

Reinforcing activities that some children might need

1   Use a collection of circle segments (figure 17). Ask the children to sort them into groups which make complete circles. (SSM3b)

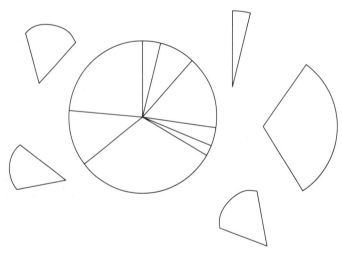

FIGURE 17 *Making circles*

2   Play turning games as a class. Start with everyone facing the same way.
If you do a half turn, what will you face? Try it.
If you do a quarter turn what will you see? Try it.
Try including left and right or clockwise and anticlockwise instructions too! (SSM3b)

Activities that some children might be ready to move on to

1   *Doors.* (SSM3c, SSM4b, UA3a)

2   *Make two circles.* (SSM3c, SSM4b, UA2a)

3   Art activities which involve rotating shapes through quarter, half and three-quarter turns and using these shapes to print with or draw round. (SSM3c)

ACTIVITY 2   # TOWERS

1   Understanding angle as a measure of turn and recognising quarter turns and half turns (e.g. giving instructions for rotating a programmable toy).
2   Asking questions, including 'What would happen if...?' and 'Why?'

What you will need

The children will need access to a Roamer, or a similar programmable robotic toy, and some building bricks or empty boxes.

What to do

Ask a group of two or three children to build a tower with the boxes/bricks. They can then place the robot as near or as far from it as they choose. Their challenge is to programme the toy to knock down the tower.

Organisation

This activity is suitable for a group of two or three children. The amount of support the teacher will need to give depends to some extent on the children's previous experience with programming the toy. Nonetheless, they will need intervention to encourage them to build on their previous experiences, rather than make a series of 'guesses':

- How will you decide what to tell the Roamer to do?
- What did you do last time?
- What happened then?
- What will you change to get closer?
- Did it turn enough? Too much?
- Did it go far enough? Too far?

While the teacher is working with this group, the rest of the children will need to be engaged in an activity which does not require his or her undivided attention.

Activities that some children might need to do first

1   Direct the Roamer to touch the wall and return to the starting place. (SSM3b)

2   Take it in turns to give each other instructions for: walking across the room, around an obstacle course, through a wood, etc. (SSM3b)

Reinforcing activities that some children might need

1   Direct the Roamer to 'park' under a chair. (SSM3b)

2   Use the graphics facility in the Logo language to write your initials. (SSM3b)

Activities that some children might be ready to move on to

1   Extend the original activity by asking the children to direct the Roamer to two or three towers and knock them down. Can they do it all in one move? (SSM3b)

2   Ask the children to draw a simple design with straight lines.
Then ask them to write instructions for their friends to follow in order to reproduce the same design. (SSM3b)

3   Direct the Roamer to walk around the edge of the classroom following the wall. (SSM3b)

4   Make two sides of a road with pencils or rulers. Make the road wide enough for the Roamer. Programme the toy to 'walk' along the road. (SSM3b)

ACTIVITY 3   TURN!

┌─────────────── LEARNING OBJECTIVES ───────────────┐

1   Understanding angle as a measure of turn and recognising quarter turns and half turns.
2   Recognising right angles.
3   Asking questions, including 'What would happen if...?' and Why?'

└──┘

What you will need

The children really need nothing at all to play this game. Teachers may choose to make some cards from the worksheet on page 57 to help them along.

What to do

The children stay at their desks or tables, but move their chairs so that they start the game all facing the same way, and standing up. A leader is chosen. (It is probably best for the teacher to be the leader for the first few tries!)

The leader calls out instructions for the others to follow. For example:

- a quarter turn to the right;
- half a turn;
- three-quarters of a turn anticlockwise.

If the children move incorrectly, they have to sit down. The last person standing is the next leader.

Organisation

This activity is a nice class game for beginning or ending a day or session. Teachers may choose to sit the children who are most likely to get in a muddle next to the ones who won't!

Activities that some children might need to do first

1 *Towers.* (SSM3b, SSM4b)

2 Play a similar game, using instructions like 'Turn to face the wall - go the long way round', 'Turn to face the back of the room - go the quick way round'.

3 Play the same game, but let the children use a set of direction cards made from the worksheet on page 58 to help them. (SSM3b)

Reinforcing activities that some children might need

1 Use a set of cards with the instructions on. Choose a leader; the leader reads the instructions for the rest of the children to follow. (SSM3b)

2 Play the same game, but the children must have their eyes closed (mind the chairs!). (SSM3b)

Activities that some children might be ready to move on to

1 Play the same game using more sophisticated instructions, e.g. 'Turn 30 degrees clockwise'. (SSM3b)

2 In pairs, write instructions for another pair of children to use to find a route across the room. (SSM3b)

ACTIVITY 4   LETTERS

+---+
| ─────────── LEARNING OBJECTIVES ─────────── |
| 1   Understanding angle as a measure of turn and recognising |
| quarter turns and half turns. |
| 2   Recognising right angles. |
| 3   Visualising and describing shapes and movements. |
| 4   Developing precision in using related geometric language. |
+---+

What you will need

The children will need a blindfold and some copies of the letter and/or shape cards on pages 59–60, cut into separate cards.

What to do

Place the cards upside down on a desk. Ask the children to work in pairs. One child chooses a card and directs the other around the shape of the letter shown on the card. The rest of the class must guess which letter is being traced out. The children will need to be encouraged to use appropriate words to describe the movements, e.g. quarter turn, between a quarter turn and a half turn, right, left, clockwise, anticlockwise, etc.

Organisation

This activity is suitable for a group or three or four children, once they are familiar with how to play. However, it works best as a class activity where two or three groups can have a turn while the rest of the class try to guess the shape.

The children improve enormously in their abilities to describe a route when this game is played 'little and often'. As they become more accomplished, they may choose to make up their own shapes rather than use the cards.

Activities that some children might need to do first

1   Make a pathway from paper with a few turns in it. The children take it in turns to be blindfolded and direct each other along the path. (SSM3b)

Reinforcing activities that some children might need

1   *Towers.* (SSM3b, UA4b)

2   Use a similar activity to the one described above but ask the children to write their instructions and give them to another group. (SSM3b)

Activities that some children might be ready to move on to

1   *Turn!* (SSM3b)

2   Devise a simple orienteering route around the school grounds for the children to follow. Keep it simple at first, with a maximum of five instructions, otherwise they seem to end up in a hedge somewhere.

ACTIVITY 5   MAKE TWO CIRCLES

┌─────────────── LEARNING OBJECTIVES ───────────────┐

1   Using right angles, fractions of a turn and later degrees to measure rotation and use the associated language.
2   Choosing and using appropriate measuring instruments.
3   Selecting and using the appropriate mathematics and materials.

└──┘

What you will need

The children will need:

- protractors;
- some large, coloured circles (plate-sized);
- rulers;
- a spinner or die with the following values: 10°, 30°, 45°, 60°, 90°, 180°.

What to do

This is a game for children to play in pairs. The aim is that they will get enjoyable practice in precision measurement.

The children take it in turns to spin the spinner or roll the dice, and then measure out the appropriate sector from one of the circles (teachers will probably need to draw attention to the fact that they need to place the centre of the protractor in the centre of the circle).

Players should try to assemble two complete circles from the sectors they make. The first player with two circles wins the game.

Organisation

This activity works well if children are playing in pairs. They will very likely need help as they begin the game and encouragement to get themselves organised. After that, the teacher will only need to pass by occasionally to offer words of encouragement as they play.

Children who are familiar with the game are often quite impressive 'teachers' themselves if they are asked to teach someone else to play.

After they get going, the players usually work quite independently, so teachers may choose to engage some of the rest of the class in an activity which requires some support, while the rest are busy with one of the activities at the end of the section, or some other reasonably independent task.

Activities that some children might need to do first

1   Using commercially produced equipment or teacher's own shapes, ask the children to make a collection of shapes, which together make 360° (see figure 18). (SSM3c)
2   Match and sort angles onto a Venn diagram, for example, into greater than and less than 90° (see figure 19). (SSM3c)

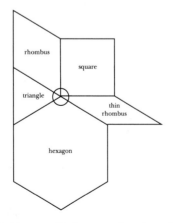

FIGURE 18 *Pattern blocks, joined to show 360º*

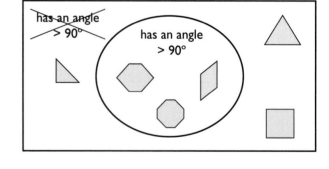

FIGURE 19 *Match and sort angles*

3   Cut a 'mouth' from a circle. Ask the children to guess how many degrees the mouth is open. Measure with a protractor to check (see figure 20). (SSM3c)

FIGURE 20
Cut a mouth from a circle

Reinforcing activities that some children might need

1   Play the game backwards, where each child starts with two circles. Whatever is rolled on the die, the children need to cut that angle out of the shape and discard it. The first player to lose all their shapes is the winner. (SSM3c)

2   Use the graphics facility in the Logo language. (SSM3c)

Activities that some children might be ready to move on to

1   Use the graphics facility in the Logo language. (SSM3c)

2   Extend the game so that children must declare what 'angle' they have left to get rid of, after each turn. (SSM3c)

ACTIVITY 6   DOORS

LEARNING OBJECTIVES
1   Using right angles, fractions of a turn and later degrees to measure rotation and use the associated language.
2   Understanding and using the language of measures.

What you will need

The children will need access to as many doors as possible in the classroom, a protractor (either a commercial one or a copy of the simple version offered on the worksheet on page 61) and some chalk. They will also need a set of cards made from the worksheet on page 61.

What to do

A group of children take it in turns to choose one of the cards, and together make one of the doors in the room mark the same angle on the floor with chalk. Ask them to fix the door open with something, and label the angle they have made.

Ask them to explain to the rest of the class what they have done, and how they did it.

- Which ones were easy to make?
- Which ones were difficult? (The children will want to discuss practical difficulties as well as mathematical ones!)

Organisation

This activity is suitable for a group of two or three children, or maybe two groups, if you have enough doors! The teacher will need to be available to support the children as they try the first couple of doors:

- How will you measure?
- Where will you show the angle?
- Which way round will you put the protractor?
- How will you hold the door open?

After that, the children can usually progress by themselves, and the teacher is then available to work with other children.

While the teacher is working with this group, the rest of the children can be engaged in one of the activities at the end of this section.

Activities that some children might need to do first

1   *Letters.* (SSM2a, SSM3a)

2   Children take it in turns to give each other instructions for: walking across the room, around an obstacle course, through a wood, etc. (SSM3c)

3   Activities involving the Roamer or some other robotic toy. (SSM3b)

Reinforcing activities that some children might need

1   *Make two circles.* (SSM3c, SSM4b, UA2a)

2   Use the graphics facility in the Logo language. (SSM3c)

Activities that some children might be ready to move on to

1   Ask the children to draw a simple design with straight lines.
Then ask them to write instructions for their friends to follow in order to reproduce the same design. (SSM3b)

2   Ask the children to use the protractor to measure other angles that they make using bent art straws, plastic Meccano or pipe cleaners. (SSM3c)

ANGLE ACTIVITIES FOR THE REST OF THE CLASS

These ideas are designed for children to use with little support from the teacher, other than initial clarification. Teachers may choose to turn them into worksheets or challenge cards, or simply to explain to the children what is expected of them.

1   Use a clock with hands that move like the hands on a real clock, rather than hands which move freely.
- Find and record five different times with an angle of 90° between the hands.
- Find and record five different times with an angle of 180° between the hands.
- Find and record five different times with an angle of 30° between the hands.
- Find and record five different times with an angle of 120° between the hands. (SSM3c)

2   Use a clock with hands that move like the hands on a real clock, rather than hands which move freely. Draw eight clocks. Put a different time on each. Find the angle between the hands at these times. (SSM3c)

3   Use a clock with hands that move like the hands on a real clock, rather than hands which move freely. Find two different times which have the same angle between the hands. Find more pairs of times. (SSM3c).

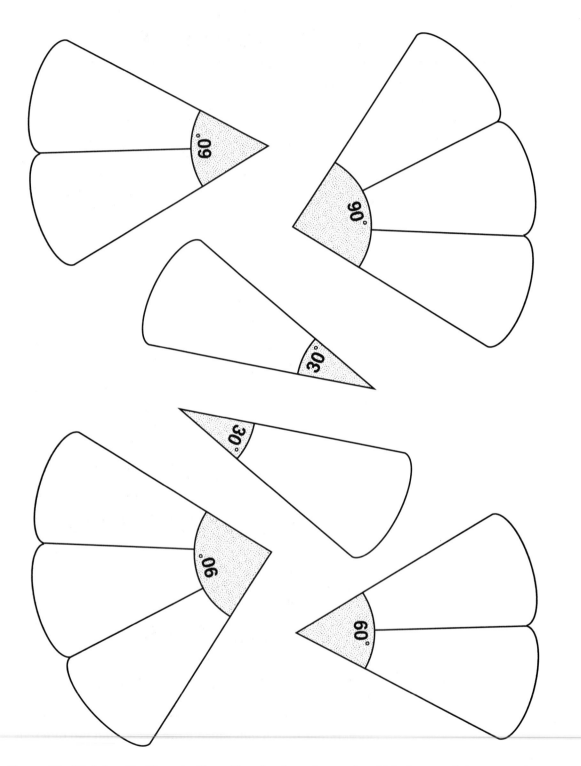

FIGURE 21 *Worksheet 1 –* Flowers. *You will need at least three copies of this sheet, made into game pieces. Hodder & Stoughton © 1996 Janine Blinko and Ann Slater Teaching Measures. The publishers grant permission for multiple copies of this worksheet to be made in the place of purchase for use solely in that institution.*

a quarter turn left
a quarter turn right
a quarter turn clockwise
a quarter turn anticlockwise
three-quarter turn left
three-quarter turn anticlockwise
a whole turn left
a whole turn right
a whole turn clockwise
a whole turn anticlockwise
a half turn left
a half turn clockwise
a half turn anticlockwise

FIGURE 22A *Worksheet 2 – Turn! 1*

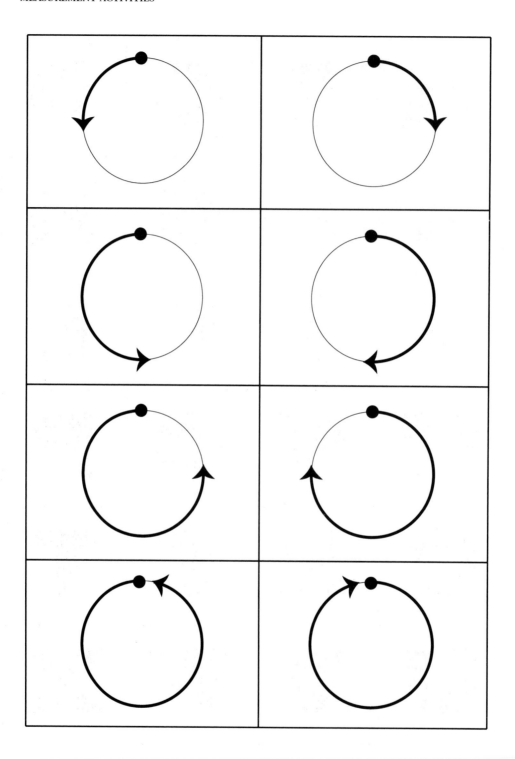

FIGURE 22B *Worksheet 3 – Turn! 2*
Hodder & Stoughton © 1996 Janine Blinko and Ann Slater Teaching Measures. The publishers grant permission for multiple copies of this worksheet to be made in the place of purchase for use solely in that institution.

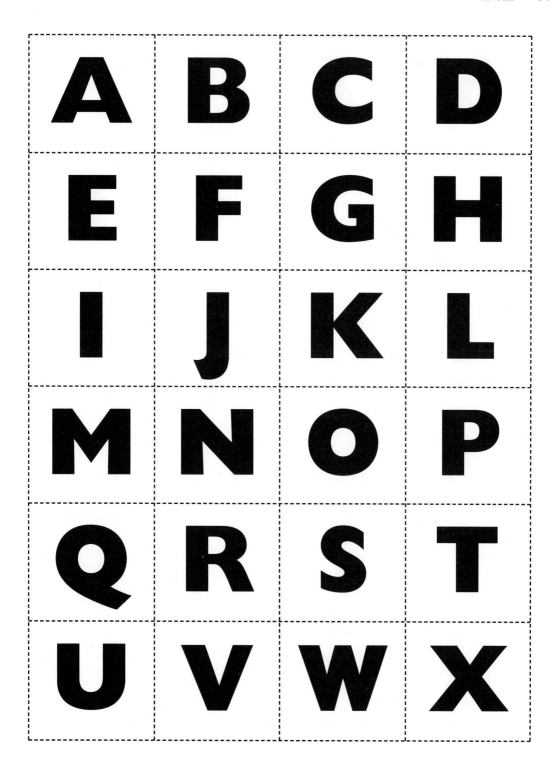

FIGURE 23A *Worksheet 4 – Letters 1*
Hodder & Stoughton © 1996 Janine Blinko and Ann Slater Teaching Measures. The publishers grant permission for multiple copies of this worksheet to be made in the place of purchase for use solely in that institution.

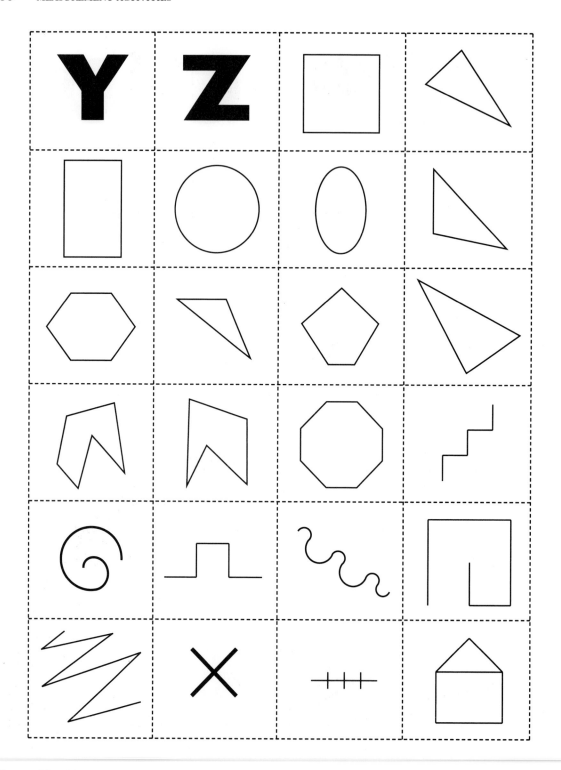

FIGURE 23B *Worksheet 5 – Letters 2*
Hodder & Stoughton © 1996 Janine Blinko and Ann Slater Teaching Measures. The publishers grant permission for multiple copies of this worksheet to be made in the place of purchase for use solely in that institution.

10°	30°	60°	135°
10°	30°	60°	135°
90°	180°	45°	5°
90°	180°	45°	5°

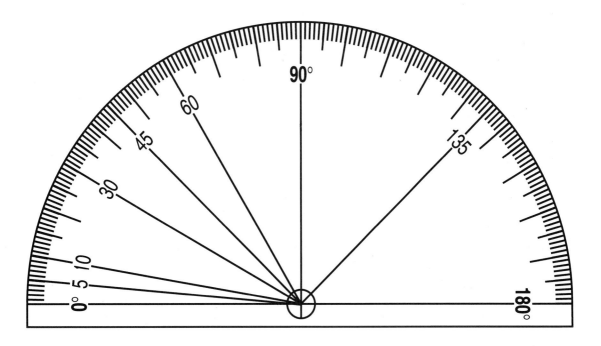

FIGURE 24 *Worksheet 6 – Doors*
Hodder & Stoughton © 1996 Janine Blinko and Ann Slater Teaching Measures. The publishers grant permission for multiple copies of this worksheet to be made in the place of purchase for use solely in that institution.

CHAPTER 6

MASS

This chapter includes:

- Introduction
- Plasticine models
- Envelopes
- Filling boxes
- Kilogram collections
- Weigh yourself
- Popcorn
- How many stones?
- Gravel balance
- Magnets
- Mass activities for the rest of the class

The problems related to this section are:

- Make a set of weights   (page 186)
- How much does your house weigh?   (page 187)
- Does the class weigh a tonne?   (page 189)
- Make a box to carry 1 kilogram   (page 189)
- Parcels   (page 190)
- Make a bag to carry 5 kilograms   (page 194)
- Invent a new way of measuring   (page 194)
- Plan a trip   (page 196)
- Plan a picnic   (page 196)
- Plan a bring-and-buy sale   (page 197)

INTRODUCTION

There are a number of 'hidden' understandings that children may need to be helped with as they learn to measure mass, and to identify the difference between mass and weight (the force exerted on something by the pull of gravity). They need to understand that:

- the concept of balance is central to the measurement of weight, and items have the same mass only if they balance;
- a balance scale can be used to match and order masses;
- an object's mass is different from its volume;
- mass is the amount of matter in an object;
- there are certain skills involved in using a balance:
  - pausing;
  - careful placements;
  - adding one by one.

The National Curriculum suggests certain goals at each Key Stage in the understanding of the measurement of mass (see figure 25).

	Pupils should be taught to:
Key Stage 1	**a** compare events using appropriate language, by direct comparison; begin to use standard units of mass, choosing units appropriate to the situation; estimate with these units
	b choose and use simple measuring instruments, reading and interpreting numbers and scales with some accuracy
Key Stage 2	**a** choose appropriate standard units of mass and make sensible estimates with them in everyday situations; extend their understanding of the relationships between units; convert one metric unit to another; know the rough metric equivalents of imperial units still in daily use
	b choose and use appropriate measuring instruments; interpret numbers and read scales to an increasing degree of accuracy

FIGURE 25 *Key Stage goals – Mass*

ACTIVITY 1 PLASTICINE MODELS

┌─────────────── LEARNING OBJECTIVES ───────────────┐

1   Comparing objects using appropriate language by direct comparison.
2   Understanding the language of comparatives.

└──┘

What you will need

The children will need plasticine (or some other modelling material) and a pan balance.

What to do

Ask the children to make two plasticine balls which weigh the same. Let the children decide how to check that both balls weigh the same. The idea that they should balance is often surprisingly difficult for them.

Once it has been established that both balls really do weigh the same, ask them to make a pancake with one and a snake with another. Discuss what they have done:

- Will they still balance?
- Why or why not?
- How do you know?
- Check it to find out.

Let them try other combinations of models of their own choice. Alternatively, make a copy of the worksheet on page 86 into a set of cards. Let the children choose two cards and make the models indicated.

Either they can start by making two balls which balance, or simply make the models and adjust them until they do balance.

Organisation

This activity works best if a group of six to eight children work individually or in pairs while the rest of the class either try one of the activities at the end of the section or are engaged in another reasonably independent task.

The teacher needs to be available as the children begin the activity, then they can usually be left to make several pairs of models which balance.

Activities that some children might need to do first

1   From a collection of interesting objects, ask the children to choose one and place it in one side of a pan balance. Let them place plasticine in the other side until it balances. (SSM4a)

2   Make coat hanger mobiles. Use wire coat hangers and a collection of reasonably small, interesting objects. (These could be things that children have made, e.g. decorations or things to do with their current topic.) (SSM4a)

Reinforcing activities that some children might need

1   Take two handfuls of cubes. Did you have the same number of cubes in each hand? Add more to the lighter side until they balance. What was the difference between the original handfuls? (SSM4a)

2   Try the same activity using other materials, such as conkers, acorns, shells or teddy bear counters. (SSM4a)

Activities that some children might be ready to move on to

1   Extend the original activity by asking the children to start with two balancing balls of plasticine, and to use one to make a single model, e.g. a cat, and the other to make two or three models, e.g. two people, three sausages, two different snakes. (SSM4a)

2   The children will need a mixed collection of objects (a 'balance box'), and some paper cups. Ask them to make pairs of cups. The cups in each pair must balance, but the contents must be different. (SSM4a)

Similar activities for other measures

LENGTH	AREA	TIME	CAPACITY/VOLUME
• *Bodies*	• *Boxes*	• *How long*	• *Sinkers*
• *Detectives*	• *Letter shapes*	• *Time lines*	• *Junk boxes*
• *Make a line*		• *Days of the week*	

ACTIVITY 2   ENVELOPES

┌─────────────────── LEARNING OBJECTIVES ───────────────────┐

1   Comparing objects using appropriate language by direct comparison.
2   Using common non-standard units of weight.
3   Understanding the language of comparatives.

└──┘

What you will need

The children will need:

• some envelopes;
• some washers, large paper clips or some other relatively heavy, flat objects.

What to do

Let the children have one envelope each, on which they put their name. Each child then:

• takes some washers (as many or as few as they like, although it is wise to give them an upper limit!);
• counts them;

- writes the number on a piece of paper and hides it in a secret place;
- puts the washers in their envelope.

Ask the children to put all the envelopes together and try to guess how many washers are in each one. They will need to have some loose washers available to help them.

Teachers may choose to play this either without or with the use of a balance.

Organisation

Teachers may choose to use this activity in one of three ways.

1   As a class and group activity, where every child makes up their own envelope, maybe with a variety of objects to use as fillers. The envelopes are then put together in a box. Groups can take it in turns to have the box and make a guess at ten of the envelopes, keeping a record of the guesses (they may need help in how to set out their records). The truth about the numbers can be revealed at a later date.

2   As a class activity where every child makes up their own envelope and then swaps with ten or more others in the class.

3   As a group activity/game where every child in the group makes up their own envelope. Then they all try to guess each others' envelopes and write their name and their guess on the other side of the envelope. The person whose guess is the closest to the actual number of washers on each envelope, gets to 'keep' it. The person with the most envelopes is the winner!

The rest of the class can be involved in either one of the activities at the end of the section or another reasonably independent task.

Activities that some children might need to do first

1   Balance two objects in their hand or on a pan balance and decide which is the heaviest/lightest. (SSM4a)

2   *Plasticine models.*

Reinforcing activities that some children might need

1   *Popcorn.*

2   Use other secret collections, e.g. cubes, conkers, paper, etc., in an envelope, in a tray, in bag. (SSM4a)

3   *Kilogram collections.*

4   *Filling boxes.*

Activities that some children might be ready to move on to

1   *Gravel balance.*

2   *How many stones?*

3   *Weigh yourself.*

Similar activities for other measures

LENGTH
- *Bodies*
- *How long*
- *Plasticine sausages*
- *Ten*

AREA
- *Cotton wool balls*
- *Vegetables*

CAPACITY/VOLUME
- *Fill a pot*

ACTIVITY 3   FILLING BOXES

┌─────────────── LEARNING OBJECTIVES ───────────────┐

1   Comparing objects using appropriate language by direct
    comparison.
2   Using common non-standard units of mass.
3   Beginning to use a wider range of standard units.
4   Selecting and using the appropriate mathematics and
    materials.

└──┘

What you will need

The children will need access to a variety of objects for filling, some
standard weights, the use of a balance and a variety of empty food
boxes, packets and tins.

What to do

Set the children the task of choosing some boxes and filling them
with anything they choose, so that they weigh the same as is
indicated on the packet.

Organisation

This activity seems to need most teacher time at the beginning, and 'passing' encouragement thereafter. The children need support in thinking through how to start. This 'thinking it out' process takes longer than most of us expect, and teachers need to have the nerve to keep quiet and wait for their ideas to come.

Teachers may choose to let the children find 'fillings' or they may decide that it is more appropriate to have a selection ready for them to choose from. Expecting them to find their own leads them to start off using heavier objects, and then doing the fine tuning with lighter objects like interlocking cubes or paper clips.

This activity usually works best with a group of six to eight working in pairs while the rest of the class either try one of the activities at the end of the section or are engaged in another reasonably independent task.

Activities some children might need to do first

1   *Kilogram collections.*

2   Use an empty box. Offer the children a variety of materials to fill it with. Set challenges, e.g. Can they fill it so that it weighs more than/less than thirty cubes? (SSM4a)

3   *Envelopes.*

Reinforcing activities that some children might need

1   *Popcorn.*

2   Use any collection of objects:
   • Can you find one object which weighs almost exactly 1 kilogram?
   • Can you find two objects which together weigh 1 kilogram? Three objects? Four? (SSM4a)

3   Try the same activities using half a kilogram as the measure. (SSM4a)

Activities that some children might be ready to move on to

1   *Gravel balance.*

2   *How many stones.*

3   Change the task so that the children need to fill the packet so that it weighs half, or twice the weight indicated on the side. Make the task more of a challenge by expecting the boxes to be full when they equal the same weight as indicated.

Let the children make a collection of these packets so that together they balance with a 5 kilogram bag of potatoes. The children either solve this problem by trial and error, or by addition. In the latter case, they may find a calculator useful. They may find that it is not possible to do this without taking a few objects out. In which case, how close can they get? (The children will need to use a bucket balance for this.) (SSM4a,b)

Similar activities for other measures

LENGTH
- *Metre mouse*
- *Ten*

AREA
- *Grids*
- *Boxes*

CAPACITY/VOLUME
- *Sinkers*
- *Blanket box*

ACTIVITY 4   # KILOGRAM COLLECTIONS

LEARNING OBJECTIVES

1 Comparing objects using appropriate language by direct comparison.
2 Using common non-standard units of mass.
3 Beginning to use a wider range of standard units.
4 Selecting and using the appropriate mathematics and materials.

What you will need

The children will need access to a variety of objects, some kilogram and half kilogram weights, and the use of a pan balance.

What to do

Set the children the task of working on their own or in pairs to make a collection of objects which together balance with 1 kilogram.

The children are usually very particular about the exactness of their collection, so it is helpful if they have access to some small objects, such as buttons, for fine tuning!

Discuss the collections that different groups have made:

- Who used the most objects?
- Who used the fewest objects?
- Who used the largest objects?
- Who used the smallest object?
- Did anyone use similar objects?
- How did you make sure your measurement was exact?

Organisation

Teachers may choose to organise the children in one of two ways; their choice may depend on the availability of equipment, the space available (as the children will probably need to move around) or on the children:

1 Let a group of six to eight children work individually or in pairs on this activity while the rest of the class try either one of the activities at the end of the section or are engaged in another reasonably independent task.

2 Let the class try the activity in groups of two or three and have a class discussion about the outcomes, or discussions with groups of children as they complete the task.

Teachers will find that they do not need to be with the children all the time as they work on this task, rather they will need to 'pass by' now and then to offer encouraging words and to be available to discuss the results when the children finish.

Activities that some children might need to do first

1 Using a collection of interesting objects of different weights, take pairs of objects and find out which is heaviest and record the results. (SSM4a)

2 Find three things heavier and three things lighter than 1 kilogram. (SSM4a)

3 *Filling boxes.*

Reinforcing activities that some children might need

1 Using the collections they have already made, set the children one of the following challenges:
- Try the same activities using half a kilogram as the measure.
- Find a way to record the collections. The children may choose to draw a graph or to sort them and record in some way.
- Ask the children to find some things that they think will weigh about 1 kilogram and to check to find out how close they are. (SSM4a)

2 *Weigh yourself.*

Activities that some children might be ready to move on to

1 *Popcorn.*

2 *How many stones?*

3 *Gravel balance.*

Similar activities for other measures

LENGTH
- Let the children draw themselves a metre. Ask them to collect objects to fit along the line exactly. Discuss the collections that different groups have made:
  - Who used the most objects?
  - Who used the fewest objects?
  - Who used the largest objects?
  - Who used the smallest object?
  - Did anyone use similar objects?
  - How did you make sure your measurement was exact?
    (SSM4a)
- *Ten*
- *Metre mouse*

AREA
- Draw a square metre, or ask the children to do it.
  Set the children the task of collecting objects, e.g. books, playing cards, boxes, paper, to fill the space exactly. The children find rulers quite useful for fine tuning! Discuss the collections that different groups have made:
  - Who used the most objects?
  - Who used the fewest objects?
  - Who used the largest objects?
  - Who used the smallest object?
  - Did anyone use similar objects?
  - How did you make sure your measurement was exact?
    (SSM4a,c)
- *Grids*
- *Boxes*

CAPACITY/VOLUME
- *Sinkers*
- *Blanket box*

ACTIVITY 5   WEIGH YOURSELF

┌─────────────────────── LEARNING OBJECTIVES ───────────────────────┐

1   Choosing appropriate standard units of mass and making
    sensible estimates with them in everyday situations.
2   Extending understanding of relationships between units;
    converting one metric unit to another.
3   Knowing the rough metric equivalent of imperial units in
    daily use; choosing and using appropriate measuring
    instruments.
4   Interpreting numbers and reading scales to an appropriate
    level of accuracy.
5   Checking results and considering whether they are sensible.

└──┘

What you will need

The children will need a pair of bathroom scales plus 'large' things
to hold, such as:

- a bag of potatoes;
- an empty schoolbag;
- a pile of books;
- a box of bricks;
- a pillow;
- a book;
- an empty carton.

What to do

- Ask the children if they know how much they weigh. Can they
  estimate (standard and/or imperial)?
- Let the group take it in turns to weigh themselves on the scales.
  Children often need help to read the scales. Teachers may feel
  that it is best to use the kilogram scale, or they may wish to use
  this opportunity to discuss the use of imperial measures and
  the relationship between metric and imperial units of measure.
  Then let them weigh themselves holding different things –
  light and heavy.

- Which things make a difference to their weight and which don't?
- Can they explain why some things have no effect on the scales?
- Leave them to classify objects into those which make a big
  difference, those which make a slight difference and those
  which make no difference to the scales.

Organisation

There are two reasons why this activity is best for just a group to try. Firstly, it takes up quite a bit of space, and secondly most teachers find it a challenge to find more than two or three sets of bathroom scales.

The children really need the teacher to be available for discussion as they begin this activity, so the rest of the class will need to be involved in one of the activities at the end of the section or another activity which requires little support from the teacher.

Activities that some children might need to do first

1   Weigh relatively 'light' objects in a pan balance using standard weights (see *Popcorn* for suggestions). (SSM4a,b)

2   Let the children weigh themselves. How many bags of potatoes would they balance with? (SSM4a)

3   Ask the children to find out the weights of everyone in their house (including the pets). Let them draw a picture of them all in order of their weights. (SSM4a)

Reinforcing activities that some children might need

1   Let the children weigh themselves on a pair of bathroom scales. Let the children weigh themselves with and without their shoes, coats, hats, sweaters. Which clothes make a difference to their weight? (SSM4a)

2   *Popcorn.*

Activities that some children might be ready to move on to

1   Let the children find out what they weigh standing, sitting, crouching, etc. Why might the results vary? Why shouldn't they? Let them discuss and suggest results first. (SSM4a)

2   *How many stones?*

3   *Gravel balance.*

Similar activities for other measures

LENGTH
- *Metre mouse*

AREA
- *Make a square metre*

CAPACITY/VOLUME
- *Sponges*
- *Blanket box*
- *Elastic bands*
- *Fill a litre*
- *200 grams of plasticine*

ACTIVITY 6   POPCORN

┌─────────────── LEARNING OBJECTIVES ───────────────┐

1   Choosing appropriate standard units of mass and making
     sensible estimates with them in everyday situations.
2   Extending understanding of relationships between units;
     converting one metric unit to another.
3   Knowing the rough metric equivalent of imperial units in
     daily use; choosing and using appropriate measuring
     instruments.
4   Interpreting numbers and reading scales to an
     appropriate level of accuracy.
5   Checking results and considering whether they are
     sensible.

└──┘

What you will need

The children will need some uncooked popping corn, and access to
some means of cooking it (either a microwave oven or a saucepan
and hob) and an adult to help them with the cooking.

What to do

Let the children experiment with popcorn. As a group, let them
weigh it before it is cooked and keep a note of the weight. Then let
them cook it and weigh it again.

- Is there a difference?
- What is the difference?
- Should there be a difference?

If you have enough popcorn, let the children try again, but this
time ask them if they can think of ways to make the experiment
easier. They frequently decide to use less popcorn to start with, as it
increases so drastically in size, and to make the starting weight an
easier value, e.g. 50 grams or 100 grams, which makes the
comparison after cooking easier to see.

Organisation

This activity can be used in one of three ways:

1   If teachers are fortunate enough to have an adult helper in the room, or an occasional parent helper, the children can work in a group with that helper, while the teacher works with the rest of the class on one of the reinforcing activities given below.

2   As a class activity where the teacher demonstrates the activity with the help of one or two of the children.

3   The teacher can work with a group while the rest of the class try either one of the activities at the end of the section or are engaged in another reasonably independent task.

Activities that some children might need to do first

1   You need a collection of reasonably light objects, e.g. pencils, crayons, small mascots, socks, etc. Let the children take it in turns to guess what an object weighs in grams and check. If they are close, they get to keep the object; if not, it goes back (the children will have to come to an agreement about what 'close' means). The winner has the most objects at the end of the game. (SSM4a)

2   Straightforward 'weighing' activities using non-standard measures, such as balancing books with cubes or conkers. (SSM4a)

Reinforcing activities that some children might need

1   Try similar experiments with other foodstuffs which visibly change, e.g. cake mix, spinach. (SSM4a)

2   Investigate fruit and vegetables by asking:
   • How many apples in a kilogram? Try other fruits.
   • How many grapes for a banana? Try other fruits. (SSM4a)

Activities that some children might be ready to move on to

1   Extend the activity by setting challenges; e.g. make a cake which weighs as near to a kilogram as possible when it is cooked. (SSM4a)

2   Extend the use of fruit and vegetables suggested in the 'reinforcing' section by asking each child to collect exactly 250 grams of fruit. Set challenges, for example:
   • You must use five different types of fruit.
   • You may only have four pieces of fruit.
     Extend the ideas even further by asking each child to cost their fruit collection using realistic prices. Similarly, set challenges:
   • If 1 kilogram of grapes is 65p, how much is a grape worth?
   • If 1 kilogram of apples is £1.29, how much is one apple? (SSM4a,b)

3   *Gravel balance.*

Similar activities for other measures

LENGTH

- *Metre mouse*

AREA

- *Make a square metre*

CAPACITY/VOLUME

- Cook popcorn as described in the original activity, but instead of comparing the weight of the popcorn before and after cooking, compare the space it takes up. Discuss with the children why and how the capacity changes.

  Teachers may feel that some children can consider changes in both weight and volume at the same time. (SSM4a)
- *Sponges*
- *Blanket box*
- *Elastic bands*
- *Fill a litre*
- *200 grams of plasticine*

ACTIVITY 7   HOW MANY STONES?

┌──────────────── LEARNING OBJECTIVES ────────────────┐

1   Choosing appropriate standard units of mass and making sensible estimates with them in everyday situations.
2   Extending understanding of relationships between units; converting one metric unit to another.
3   Choosing and using appropriate measuring instruments.
4   Interpreting numbers and reading scales to an appropriate level of accuracy.
5   Trying different mathematical approaches.
6   Identifying and obtaining information needed to carry out work.

└───┘

What you will need

The children will need:

- a pan balance;
- some weights;
- some pea shingle or gravel (the type used in fish tanks is pretty and reasonably priced);
- some paper bags.

What to do

Let each child in a group:

- take some gravel in one hand and put it in a bag;
- guess how much their bags weigh in grams;
- weigh them as accurately as possible;
- write the weight on the bag in big numbers and letters.

Discuss the outcomes with the children:

- Whose weighs the most? Least?
- Can you put them in order?

(Many children will be able to answer these questions by looking at the numbers, but it is essential that the answers are checked on a balance.)

- How many stones are there in each handful?

Let the children count and record the number of stones by writing on the other side of their bag.

- Who had the most stones? Fewest?
- Did the person who had the heaviest bag also have the most stones?
- Can you put the bags in order according to the number of stones they contain?
- Is the order the same as before?

Leave the children to fill their own set of six bags with different amounts of gravel and label them.

Organisation

The first part of this activity is quite teacher-intensive, as the children will need support in the discussion about their bags. It is probably easiest to work with six to eight children as a group while the rest of the class try either one of the activities at the end of the section or are engaged in another reasonably independent task.

Activities that some children might need to do first

1   You need a collection of reasonably light objects, e.g. pencils, crayons, small mascots, socks, etc. Let the children take it in turns to guess what an object weighs in grams and check. If they are close, they get to keep the object; if not, it goes back (the children will have to come to an agreement about what 'close' means). The winner has the most objects at the end of the game. (SSM4a,b)

2   Straightforward 'weighing' activities using non-standard measures such as balancing books with cubes or conkers. (SSM4a)

Reinforcing activities that some children might need

1   Ask the children to take about 10 grams of stones and put them in a bag. Let them check. Try 20 grams' worth, 30 grams, etc. (SSM4a,b)

2   *Kilogram collections.*

3   *Filling boxes.*

Activities that some children might be ready to move on to

1   Fill two bags with different amounts of stones. Find their weight in grams and/or the number of stones. Find the average weight and/or the average number of stones. Change them so that they still balance. Try three bags! (SSM4a,b)

2   *Gravel balance.*

Similar activities for other measures

LENGTH
*   The children will need an assortment of string, paper and ribbon of different lengths. Let all the children in a group take a length, measure it and attach a label to it. Discuss the outcomes with the children:
    – Whose is the longest? Shortest?
    – Can you put them in order?
    (Many children will be able to answer these questions by looking at the numbers, but it is essential that the answers are checked practically.)
        Leave the children to choose their own set of lengths to measure and label. Ask them to put them in order. (SSM4a)
*   *Metre mouse*

AREA
*   *Make a square metre*

CAPACITY/VOLUME

- The children will need containers, such as yoghurt pots and small boxes (they will need to be quite different in size), gravel or pea shingle to fill them with and some measuring cups. Let all the children in a group choose a container, fill it with gravel and measure how much they have used in the measuring cup. Ask them to label their container with how much it will hold.

  Discuss the outcomes with the children:

  – Whose container held the most? Least?

  – Can you put them in order?

  (Many children will be able to answer these questions by looking at the numbers, but it is essential that the answers are checked using several identical measuring cups.)

  – How many stones are there in each container?

    Let the children count and record the number of stones by writing on the other side of their container.

  – Who had the most stones? Fewest?

  – Did the person whose container held the most also have the most stones?

  – Can you put the containers in order according to the number of stones they contain?

  – Is the order the same as before?

    Leave the children to fill their own set of six containers with different amounts of gravel and label them. (SSM4a)

- *Sponges*
- *Blanket box*
- *Elastic bands*
- *Fill a litre*
- *200 grams of plasticine*

ACTIVITY 8   GRAVEL BALANCE

┌─────────────────── LEARNING OBJECTIVES ───────────────────┐

1   Choosing appropriate standard units of mass, extending understanding of relationships between units.

2   Converting one metric unit to another.

3   Choosing and using appropriate measuring instruments.

4   Interpreting numbers and reading scales to an appropriate level of accuracy.

5   Understanding the language of measure.

└───┘

What you will need

The children will need:

- two pan balances (with good-sized pans!);
- some weights;
- some gravel (the type used in fish tanks is pretty and reasonably priced);
- a spinner or dice with the following values: 250 grams, 200 grams, 150 grams, 100 grams, 50 grams, 0.

What to do

This is a game for children to play in pairs. The aim is that children will get enjoyable practice in precision measurement.

Players must decide on one of the balances as the one where they keep their collections of gravel, and they must identify one side of the balance as 'theirs' for the game. The other is for use during play. The children take it in turns to:

- spin the spinner or roll the dice;
- measure out the appropriate amount of gravel;
- pour it into their collecting pan.

The winner of the game has the heaviest side after five rounds of the game.

Organisation

The children will need a reasonable amount of space as they play this game. Teachers may find it best to find the players a space at the side of the classroom where they will not be disturbed. They will very likely need help as they begin the game, and encouragement to get themselves organised. After that, the teacher will only need to pass by occasionally to offer words of encouragement as they play.

Children who are familiar with the game are often quite impressive 'teachers' themselves if they are asked to teach someone else to play.

Because of the space and equipment needed, it usually works best if two, or at most four, children play. After they get going, the players usually work quite independently, so teachers may choose to engage some of the rest of the class in an activity which requires some support, such as *Popcorn*, while the rest are busy with one of the activities at the end of the section or some other reasonably independent task.

Activities that some children might need to do first

1 Place objects (e.g. a shoe, a teddy, a big shell) in one side of a pan balance, and pour gravel or sand into the other side to make it balance. (SSM4a)

2 Play the same game, but as each player spins a number, ask them to use the actual weights, rather than gravel, to put in their side of the pan. (SSM4a,b)

3 *How many stones?*

Reinforcing activities that some children might need

1 *Kilogram collections.*

2 *Filling boxes.*

3 Play the same game, but the players have their own balance. They place weights to the value of 1.5 kilograms in one side. The winner is the first player to make their pans balance by collecting gravel in the same way as before. (SSM4a,b)

Activities that some children might be ready to move on to

1 Ask players to keep a running total as they play the game. They may need a calculator to help. (SSM4a,b)

Similar activities for other measures

LENGTH
- The children will need:
  - strips of paper, string or ribbon;
  - scissors and tape;
  - a spinner or dice with the following: 0 cm, 5 cm, 10 cm, 15 cm, 20 cm, 25 cm;
  - a metre stick with centimetres marked.

  The children take it in turns to:
  - spin the spinner or roll the dice;
  - measure and cut the appropriate length of paper;
  - stick it to any they have collected previously.

  The winner of the game has the longest strip after five rounds of the game, or is the first to make 2 metres. (SSM4a,b)
- *Metre mouse*

AREA
- The children will need:
  - centimetre-squared paper;
  - scissors and tape;
  - a spinner or dice with the following: 0 cm^2, 50 cm^2, 100 cm^2, 150 cm^2, 200 cm^2, 250 cm^2.

The children take it in turns to:
- spin the spinner or roll the dice;
- measure and cut the appropriate area from their squares of paper;
- stick it to any they have collected previously.

The winner of the game has the greatest area after five rounds of the game, or is the first to make a square metre. (SSM4a,b)

- *Make a square metre*

CAPACITY/VOLUME

- The children will need:
  - a large plastic container each (both the same, to hold more than 1.5 litres!);
  - a measuring jug;
  - a spinner or dice with the following: 0 ml, 50 ml, 100 ml, 150 ml, 200 ml, 250 ml;
  - water or sand.

  The children take it in turns to:
  - spin the spinner or roll the dice;
  - measure out the appropriate amount of water;
  - pour it into their plastic container.

  The winner of the game has the most water after five rounds of the game, or is the first to make 1.5 litres. (SSM4a,b)

- *Sponges*
- *Blanket box*
- *Elastic bands*
- *Fill a litre*
- *200 grams of plasticine*

ACTIVITY 9   MAGNETS

LEARNING OBJECTIVES

1 Choosing appropriate standard units of mass and making sensible estimates with them in everyday situations.
2 Extending understanding of the relationships between units; converting one metric unit to another.
3 Knowing the rough metric equivalent of imperial units in daily use.
4 Choosing and using appropriate measuring instruments.
5 Interpreting numbers and reading scales to an appropriate level of accuracy.
6 Explaining reasoning.

What you will need

The children will need a selection of magnets of different sizes and strengths, and a collection of metal objects, some of which can be picked up by a magnet and some of which cannot.

What to do

object	weight

FIGURE 26 *Recording measurements.*

The metal objects need to be in a fairly large, flat box or spread out on the table. Ask the children to choose a magnet and use it to pick up as many things as they can.

Ask them to weigh their groups of objects either in standard or non-standard units. Teachers may wish the children to keep a record of their measurements on a chart such as Figure 26.

Discuss the outcomes with the children:

- Does the heaviest group also make the longest line?
- Does the heaviest group also contain the most objects?
- Does any group weigh more than 250 grams?
- Did the biggest magnet pick up the most objects?
- Did the smallest magnet pick up the lightest load?

Organisation

This activity usually works best with a group of six to eight working in pairs while the rest of the class try either one of the activities at the end of the section or are engaged in another reasonably independent task.

Activities that some children might need to do first

1   *Plasticine models.*

2   *Envelopes.*

Reinforcing activities that some children might need

1   *Kilogram collections.*

2   *How many stones?*

Activities that some children might be ready to move on to

1   *Filling boxes.*

2   *Gravel balance.*

Similar activities for other measures

LENGTH
- *How high?*

AREA
- *Grids*
- *Make a square metre*

CAPACITY/VOLUME
- *Sponges*
- *Blanket box*
- *Fill a litre*

MASS ACTIVITIES FOR THE REST OF THE CLASS

These ideas are designed for children to use with little support from the teacher, other than initial clarification. Teachers may choose to turn them into worksheets or challenge cards, or simply to explain to the children what is expected of them. Some activities are appropriate for a group to work on, others can be used with a whole class.

1   Make a collection of anything that together balances with: your shoe, a handkerchief, a lunch box. Draw what you have used. (SSM4a)

2   Use an empty box. Choose from a variety of materials to fill it with. Fill it so that it weighs exactly 1 kilogram. Record the contents. (SSM4a)

3   Find five things that you think will weigh about 1 kilogram. Record what they weigh. Put them in order of how close they were to weighing 1 kilogram. (SSM4a)

4   Use a collection of interesting objects of different weights. Take pairs of objects and find out which is heaviest and record. (SSM4a)

5   Make a small collection of boxes wrapped up like presents, and containing different things (washers, polystyrene, clay, etc.). Pick up two: guess, check and record which is the heaviest. Then pick up two, order them, and find another which is between the original two in weight (if there is one!). Order all the parcels and record. Balance each of them with cubes and record. (SSM4a)

6   Find a favourite cuddly toy (or something relevant to the class topic).
- How many pasta shells balance with it?
- How many paperclips?
- How many beans? Washers?

Make a graph to show what you have found out. (SSM4a)

7   Use collections of small objects, e.g. washers, counters, paper clips, cubes, polystyrene, beans, pasta, conkers. Place some washers in one pan and some counters in the other. Jiggle until they balance. Record. Find other sets of things which balance. (SSM4a)

a football	a man
a sausage	a mouse
a car	a tree
a dog	a bowl
a pig	a hat

FIGURE 27 *Worksheet 11 – Plasticine models*
Hodder & Stoughton © 1996 Janine Blinko and Ann Slater Teaching Measures. The publishers grant permission for multiple copies of this worksheet to be made in the place of purchase for use solely in that institution.

CHAPTER

CAPACITY/VOLUME

This chapter includes:

- Introduction
- Paint
- Fill a pot
- Sinkers
- Junk boxes
- Sponges
- Blanket box
- Body parts
- Elastic bands
- Fill a litre
- 200 grams of plasticine
- Guess which box
- Cones
- Floor plans
- Capacity/Volume activities for the rest of the class

The problems related to this section are:

Capacity
- How much water will fill up the classroom?   (page 186)
- How much do you drink in a day?   (page 188)
- Dripping tap   (page 188)
- Does the class weigh a tonne?   (page 189)
- Make a bag to carry 5 kilograms   (page 194)
- Invent a new way of measuring   (page 194)
- Plan a trip   (page 196)
- Plan a picnic   (page 196)
- Plan a bring-and-buy sale   (page 197)

Volume
- How much water will fill up the classroom?   (page 186)
- Make a set of weights   (page 186)
- How much does your house weigh?   (page 187)
- Make a box to hold 1 kilogram   (page 189)
- How many vital statistics can you find out about your body?   (page 191)
- Invent a new way of measuring   (page 194)
- Make a clock   (page 198)

INTRODUCTION

There are a number of 'hidden' understandings that children may need to be helped with as they learn to measure in three dimensions, and to distinguish between the space something takes up (volume) and what it will hold (capacity). They must understand that, for capacity:

- a container is only full when it holds as much as it possibly can;
- if the contents of one container are being emptied into another, the comparison or measurement is not accurate unless nothing at all has been spilled. If something is spilled, the pouring needs to be repeated;
- liquid and dry materials can be used to compare and order materials by capacity;
- a container's capacity is different from its height;
- a quantity of liquid or dry material in a container is different from the level.

For volume, they must understand that:

- in order to measure or compare volumes, the measuring unit needs to be used to fill a container as tightly as possible;
- containers can be compared and ordered by their volume;
- regular volumes have three dimensions;
- an equal number of cubes can be arranged to make different shaped buildings;
- irregular volumes can be measured by water displacement.

The National Curriculum suggests certain goals at each Key Stage in the understanding of the measurement of volume and capacity (see figure 28).

	Pupils should be taught to:
Key Stage 1	a compare objects and events using appropriate language, by direct comparison and then using common non-standard and standard units of capacity, e.g. 'about three beakers full'; begin to use a wider range of standard units, choosing units appropriate to the situation; estimate with these units b choose and use simple measuring instruments, reading and interpreting numbers and scales with some accuracy
Key Stage 2	b choose and use appropriate measuring instruments; interpret numbers and read scales to an increasing degree of accuracy
	c find areas and volumes by counting methods, leading to the use of other practical methods, e.g. dissection

FIGURE 28 *Key Stage goals – Capacity/Volume*

ACTIVITY 1 # PAINT

┌─────────────── LEARNING OBJECTIVES ───────────────┐

1 Comparing objects by direct comparison and using non-standard units.
2 Developing different mathematical approaches and looking for ways to overcome difficulties.

└──┘

What you will need

The children will need:

- some very thick paint;
- one or two small containers (e.g. a fromage frais pot);
- some water;
- some paper.

What to do

- Let one of the children in a group paint a line on one side of the paper.
- Ask someone to add one potful of water to the paint and mix it in.
- Ask the children if they think the water will change the paint in any way.
- Let another child paint another line next to the first.
- Discuss with the children any variations there might be in the colour and why that might be so.
- Repeat this until the paint is really too diluted to see.
- Expect the children to develop their use of words like 'lighter' and 'darker', and maybe even 'dilute'.
- Ask them to make some kind of record of the number of potfuls of water in each stripe.

Organisation

This activity can work well either as a class lesson, with the paper fastened to an easel so that everyone in the class can see, or as a group activity. The children probably get more out of it if they are working in a smaller group, so that each child can have a turn at mixing, painting and participating in the discussion about how the paint is changing. In this case, the rest of the class needs to be engaged in one of the activities at the end of the section or some other task which means they can work independently of the teacher.

Activities that some children might need to do first

1   Simple pouring and filling activities which involve them in discussion about 'fullness'. (SSM4a)

2   Real or pretend tea parties. (SSM4a)

3   Games that arise from turning the 'home corner' into a restaurant. (SSM4a)

Reinforcing activities that some children might need

1   Let the children make up some orange squash of different strengths, e.g. one capful of squash to a cup of water, two capfuls, three capfuls, etc. Discuss what difference they might find in the taste. Let them decide which they prefer. (SSM4a)

2   Let the children pretend to be doctors. You will need some different coloured paint which is quite thin and runny, and some plastic bottles. Let them, or the teacher, write 'prescriptions', e.g. two potfuls of green, one potful of yellow, three potfuls of blue for Sam. Let the children mix them up and put labels on them. (SSM4a)

Activities that some children might be ready to move on to

1   *Fill a pot.*

2   *Sinkers.*

3   *Elastic bands.*

Similar activities for other measures

LENGTH	AREA	WEIGHT
• *Beads*	• *Body prints*	• *Envelopes*
• *Ten*	• *Body measures*	
• *Sorting box*	• *Cotton wool balls*	
	• *Shadows*	
	• *Boxes*	
	• *Letter shapes*	

ACTIVITY 2   FILL A POT

┌─── LEARNING OBJECTIVES ───┐

1   Comparing objects by direct comparison and using non-standard units, estimating with these units.
2   Understanding the language of comparatives.

What you will need

The children will need:

- a small pot;
- a large pot (at least fifteen times bigger);
- water or sand.

What to do

This is a game for two or three players. Players take it in turns to pour one, two or three small potfuls into the large pot. The player who fills the jug with their turn wins the game.

Children will need to pay attention to, and make up rules about, spillages, and about whether players must fill the large pot *exactly* with their turn, rather than have any sand or water left over.

As the children become familiar with the game, the teacher may wish to discuss the outcomes with them:

- How many potfuls does the big container hold?
- Does it matter how many potfuls you put in each time?
- Is there a way to win every time?

Organisation

Because of the amount of equipment and the use of sand or water, this activity probably works best as a group activity, with the children working in pairs, while the rest of the class is engaged in one of the activities at the end of the section or another activity that they can work at reasonably independently.

Activities that some children might need to do first

1   Change the original game so that players have an identical large container each. One pot is chosen as the pouring pot. They take it in turns to roll a die and pour in that many potfuls from the pouring pot. The first player with a full container wins the game. (SSM4a)

2   Find a large container and a small one. Fill the large one by filling the small one and emptying the contents into it. Let the children decide how to keep count. They may decide to do this in one of two ways:
    - use the correct number of identical pots;
    - use one pot over and over.
Choose a different large container. Guess and count how many small potfuls will fit into this one. Do this every day for two weeks. Do they get better at guessing? (SSM4a)

3   *Paint.*

Reinforcing activities that some children might need

1 Ask the children to make their own calibrated container by marking the large container every time another small containerful is added. (Stick masking tape on the container to write on.)

Use the calibrations to find out how many small potfuls other containers will hold. Check by pouring cupfuls in as well. (SSM4a)

2 *Elastic bands.*

Activities that some children might be ready to move on to

1 Use a spinner with different quantities on, e.g. 150 millilitres, 20 millilitres, etc. Players take it in turns to spin, measure and pour liquid into their own jug. The first player to fill their jug or to make a litre wins the game. (SSM4a,b)

2 *Sponges.*

3 *Fill a litre.*

Similar activities for other measures

LENGTH
- The children will need some short things, e.g. matchsticks or paper clips, and a long thing (at least fifteen times longer), e.g. a piece of ribbon. This is a game for two or three players. Players take it in turns to place one, two or three small objects alongside the long one. The player whose short objects match the long one exactly with their turn wins the game.

  As the children become familiar with the game, the teacher may wish to discuss the outcomes with them:
  – How many short things match with the long one?
  – Does it matter how many small ones you put in each time?
  – Is there a way to win every time? (SSM4a)
- *Beads*
- *Ten*

AREA
- *Body prints*
- *Body measures*
- *Cotton wool balls*
- *Shadows*
- *Boxes*
- *Letter shapes*

MASS
- The children will need some light things, e.g. matchsticks, paper clips, acorns, a heavy thing, (at least fifteen times heavier), e.g. a big stone, a shoe, and a pan balance. This is a game for two or three players. The heavy object is placed in one side of the balance.

Players take it in turns to place one, two or three light objects in the other side. The player whose light objects make the two pairs balance exactly with their turn wins the game.

As the children become familiar with the game, the teacher may wish to discuss the outcomes with them:
– How many light things match with the heavy one?
– Does it matter how many light ones you put in each time?
– Is there a way to win every time? (SSM4a)

• *Envelopes*

ACTIVITY 3   SINKERS

┌─────────────── LEARNING OBJECTIVES ───────────────┐

1   Comparing objects using the appropriate language by direct comparison and using non-standard units.
2   Understanding the language of comparatives.

└──┘

What you will need

The children will need:

• two transparent pots exactly the same (the pots will need to be chosen carefully; they should not be too wide, and if possible have straight sides);
• some objects that will sink, e.g. marbles, washers.

What to do

Ask the children to fill both the pots with water to the same level. It is best if the level is marked with an elastic band. Ask them to add a 'sinker' to one. What happens? Try five sinkers. Add an identical number of sinkers to the other. What happens? Try adding different sinkers to each.

After some experimenting, half fill the container with water and let the children take it in turns to:

• mark a new level on the container;
• guess how many sinkers would be needed to raise the water level to the mark;
• try it.

Whoever has the closest guess can make the next mark.

Organisation

This activity is most suitable for a small group. When they have first been introduced to the idea of sinkers, the children can be left to experiment with the idea. They need a little teacher input when they are introduced to the main activity, and then they can be left to work on their own again while they play this simple game a few times.

The rest of the class can either be organised to work on a similar activity, for which the teacher is available for most of the time, or can be organised into groups, where one of the groups requires the teacher's attention at the outset, and the others are engaged in an activity which requires little of the teacher's time.

Activities that some children might need to do first

1   Fill a large container with water. Use a collection of objects which will sink. Let the children place the objects in the water one at a time, and mark the levels. Which changes the level most? Least? Why? (SSM4a)

2   *Fill a pot.*

Reinforcing activities that some children might need

1   • Use three pots the same. You will also need some stones of different sizes and some elastic bands.
   • Fill each pot with water to the same level.
   • Add one stone to each pot.
   • Mark the new level with elastic bands.
   • Compare and order the pots by water level.
   • Extend to ordering a collection of four, five or six stones in this way. (SSM4a)

Activities that some children might be ready to move on to

1   Fill a calibrated measuring jug to 250 millilitres. Drop in centimetre cubes. Do it again...and again and so on. Can you draw any conclusions? (SSM4a,b)

2   *Elastic bands.*

3   *Body parts.*

Similar activities for other measures

LENGTH	AREA	WEIGHT
• *Beads*	• *Body prints*	• *Envelopes*
• *Ten*	• *Body measures*	
	• *Cotton wool balls*	
	• *Shadows*	
	• *Boxes*	
	• *Letter shapes*	

ACTIVITY 4 JUNK BOXES

> 1 Comparing objects using the appropriate language by direct comparison then using non-standard units.
> 2 Understanding the language of comparatives.

What you will need

The children will need access to:

- a lot of boxes (there needs to be at least two of every type of box);
- scissors and glue.

What to do

Ask the children to find two sets of identical junk boxes or cartons. Ask them to use their collection to make two models. They will need to use one set of boxes to make each one. Ask them to make their models as different as possible. Discuss with them the differences there might be; one could be taller than the other, one could be wider, more wobbly, etc. Discuss their models with them as they are making them, and when they have finished them.

Organisation

This activity works well as a group activity, but does not require a great deal of teacher input, so the teacher will probably be able to work with another group in the class, provided he or she can 'escape' to discuss the models with the children during their construction and after they are complete.

The rest of the class will need to be engaged in one of the activities at the end of this section or some other task which requires little teacher input.

Activities that some children might need to do first

1 *200 grams of plasticine.*

2 Make five different models with fifteen interlocking cubes in each. (SSM4a)

Reinforcing activities that some children might need

1   Ask the children to find out how many boxes will fit:
   - inside a big box;
   - under the table;
   - in the sink;
   - in the cupboard, etc.

   Make them fit as closely as possible. At the simplest level, this is just a 'filling space' task. (SSM4a,c)

2   Use two identical sets of junk boxes. Use one set to make the tallest tower possible. Use the other to make the shortest tower possible. (SSM4a,c)

3   *Guess which box.*

Activities that some children might be ready to move on to

1   Let a group of children use clay to make some pots. When they are dry, ask the children to find out which holds the most sand. Can they put the pots in order according to how much they will hold? (SSM4a)

2   Let the children use boxes to make a collection of capacity measures. (SSM4a)

3   *Blanket box.*

ACTIVITY 5   SPONGES

┌─────────────── LEARNING OBJECTIVES ───────────────┐

1   Choosing appropriate standard units of capacity and making sensible estimates with them in everyday situations.
2   Presenting information and results clearly, and explaining the reasons for the choice of presentation.

└──┘

What you will need

The children will need a collection of different sponges and some capacity measures.

What to do

Ask the children to find out how much water the sponges will hold. The children will need to devise a 'fair test' and consider the following:

- Is a dripping sponge allowed?
- How many times can the sponge be squeezed to get the water out?
- How many times should each sponge be tested?
- Should the sponge be dry before the test begins?

When they have finished, ask the children to record their findings. They may decide to do so in words, pictures or on a graph (see figure 29). Discuss the outcomes with them:

- Which held the most water?
- Did you think that one would hold the most?
- Did the largest sponge hold the most water?
- Did the smallest hold the least?
- What do you think it is about a sponge that makes it a good water holder?

It is not particularly important which of the sponges holds the most water, but the quest to find out involves the children in the notion of fair testing, the use of standard capacity measure, the comparison of capacities and a consideration of the properties of materials.

FIGURE 29 *Recording findings*

Organisation

This is quite a damp activity, with plenty of drips and splashes. The children will need to be wearing appropriate clothing.

The activity works best with a group of three or four children co-operating to test a collection of sponges.

Once several groups have tested and documented their results, the results can be compared and anomalies discussed. The children will probably want to do a 'once and for all' test to iron out any of the discrepancies between results.

The actual testing does not take very long. Groups can move on to produce a 'best' copy of their results. It is quite helpful to have one of the activities listed at the end of the section running alongside this one, so that when children are not involved in testing or recording, there is something for them to do.

Activities that some children might need to do first

1   Change the activity so that the children do not need to take actual measurements, but can order the sponges by squeezing their contents into a set of identical containers, e.g. yoghurt pots, and comparing the results. (SSM4a)

2   Order the contents of a variety of containers by their contents. (SSM4a)

3   *Sinkers.*

4   *Fill a pot.*

Reinforcing activities that some children might need

1   Compare the water held in a variety of materials: a sock, a roll of cotton wool, a cloth, a tea towel, etc., and record the results. (SSM4a)

2   *Cones.*

Activities that some children might be ready to move on to

1   Test for absorbency. Hang a range of materials in a tray of water, e.g. kitchen roll, cotton wool, cotton, a tea towel, etc. Which soaks up the most? How much? Which takes the longest to soak? (SSM4a)

Similar activities for other measures

LENGTH	AREA	WEIGHT
• *Metre mouse*	• *Make a square metre*	• *Envelopes*
• *How high?*		• *Popcorn*
		• *How many stones?*
		• *Gravel balance*

ACTIVITY **6**   # BLANKET BOX

┌─ LEARNING OBJECTIVES ─┐

1 Choosing appropriate standard units of volume and making sensible estimates with them in everyday situations.
2 Extending understanding of the relationships between units.
3 Selecting and using the appropriate mathematics and materials.

What you will need

The children will need:

- plenty of metre sticks;
- masking tape;
- an old sheet or blanket;
- balloons;
- old newspapers.

What to do

Ask the children to make a cubic metre with metre sticks – this is not easy! They will need help with joining the corners with masking tape. The cubic metre will probably need support from a desk or wall. When it is finished, get them to hang a blanket over it (see figure 30).

How many children can get inside? Let the children find out...carefully! Get them to work together to find out the answers to the questions in figure 31. The children will find some discussion helpful as they work on these problems:

- How will you find out the answer?
- Do you have enough?
- How will you keep them in?

Organisation

This activity may require a reasonable amount of input from the teacher at the start, as the metre sticks are a bit wobbly. Alternatively, the teacher can leave the children to it and intervene on request.

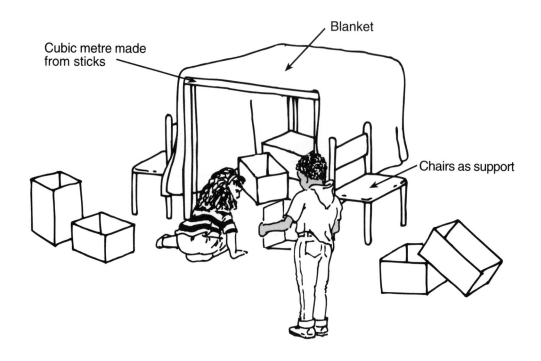

FIGURE 30 *Creating a cubic metre*

Whilst the teacher's presence is not required all the time, the children may need help and supportive suggestions along the way. The rest of the class need not be working entirely independently of the teacher, but the teacher will find that he or she needs to give this metre group some attention as they need it.

Activities that some children might need to do first

1   *Boxes.*

2   Find the capacities of boxes in a variety of non-standard units: cubes, conkers, ping-pong balls, etc. (SSM4a)

3   *Junk boxes.*

Reinforcing activities that some children might need

1   You will need a lot of used boxes and cartons. Ask the children to glue them together to make as close to a cubic metre as they can. (SSM4a)

Activities that some children might be ready to move on to

1 Ask the children to use rolled up newspaper to make a metre cube. Can they make it any shape but a cube, but still be sure it is one metre cube in 'volume'? Offer suggestions about children's methods of solving this challenge and recording what they do. Ask the children questions such as those in Figure 31. Ask the children to think up some questions of their own.(SSM4a)

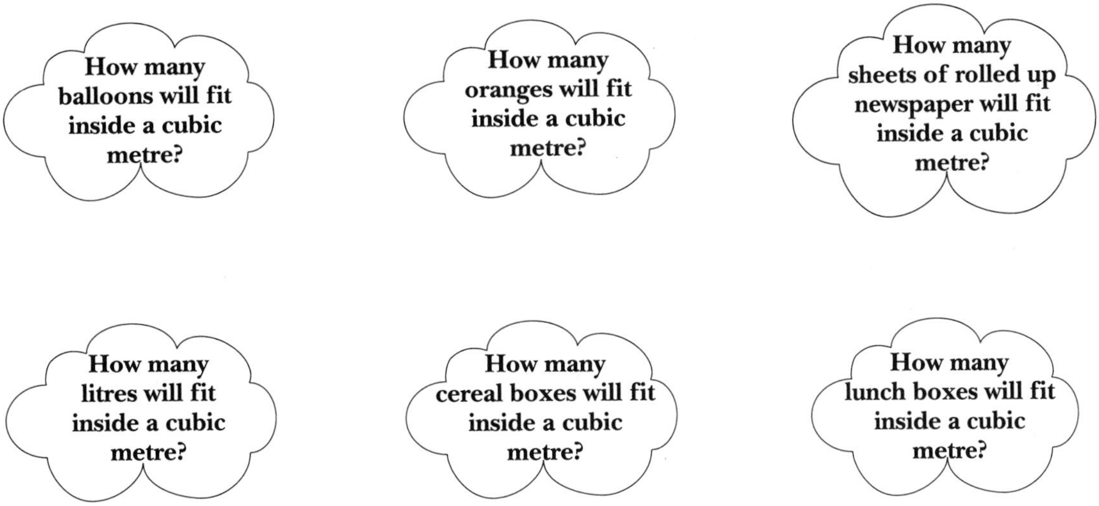

How many balloons will fit inside a cubic metre?

How many oranges will fit inside a cubic metre?

How many sheets of rolled up newspaper will fit inside a cubic metre?

How many litres will fit inside a cubic metre?

How many cereal boxes will fit inside a cubic metre?

How many lunch boxes will fit inside a cubic metre?

FIGURE 31 *Cubic metre*

2 Extend to asking the children to find out how many cubes are needed to fill a cubic metre. (SSM4a)

3 *Guess which box.*

Similar activities for other measures

LENGTH
- *Metre mouse*
- *How high?*

AREA
- *Make a square metre*

WEIGHT
- *Weigh yourself*
- *Popcorn*
- *How many stones?*
- *Gravel balance*

ACTIVITY 7 BODY PARTS

LEARNING OBJECTIVES

1 Comparing objects using appropriate language by direct comparison.
2 Using common non-standard units of volume.
3 Understanding and using the language of comparatives.

What you will need

The children need access to:

- a large container with water in, e.g. a paddling pool, a fish tank;
- some towels;
- a waterproof pen.

What to do

Ask the children to find out how much space different parts of their body take up. For example, hand, forearm, upper arm, one finger, lower leg, foot, fist, etc.

This is a comparative displacement activity, where the children use the tank of water and put bits of their bodies in. Ask them to record the water level on the side of the container. Once they have had a few tries, they can be asked to estimate whether or not the next part will make the level rise more or less than the previous part they tested.

Ask a group to choose one person in the group, and to measure various bits of that person's body and make comparisons.

- Which takes up more space, a foot or an arm?
- Why does the level change?
- Do two feet take up about the same space as two hands?
- Put the body bits in order of the space they take up.

Let the children discuss and agree a way to record their findings (see figure 32).

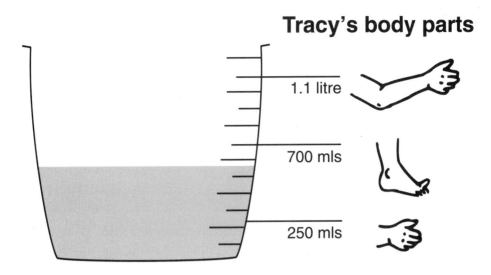

Tracy's body parts

1.1 litre

700 mls

250 mls

FIGURE 32 *A way of recording*

Organisation

The children really need supervision for this activity, if they are to get the most from the discussion, and to begin to develop an understanding of displacement. They will need a reasonable space to work in, and, ideally, to be able to work on a floor which is not carpeted, because there are always plenty of drips! Or, if the day is just right, they could work outside!

The rest of the class will need to be engaged in one of the activities at the end of the section or some other reasonably independent task.

Activities that some children might need to do first

1   *Paint.*

2   *Sinkers.*

3   *Fill a pot.*

Reinforcing activities that some children might need

1   Try the same activity as described above, but ask the children to measure the displacement caused by each foot in the group and compare. Whose foot takes up the most space? (SSM4a)

2   *Elastic bands.*

3   *Fill a litre.*

Activities that some children might be ready to move on to

1   Extend the activity described above by asking the children to make actual measurements in litres and centilitres. They usually do this by marking the water level on the side of the tank and then 'topping up the tank' with liquid, and keeping track of how much they needed. (SSM4a)

2   Extend to other parts of the body, e.g. thigh, asking the children to find their own methods of solving the problem. This might be an activity for the children to try at home in their own bath! (SSM4a)

Similar activities for other measures

LENGTH

*   Change the activity described above by asking the children to find out how many different lengths they can find on their body. They can either cut string the same length as their arm, leg, foot, hand, etc. and compare, or make measurements in centimetres and compare numbers.

     Extend to asking them how many different circumferences they can find on their body, e.g. wrist, thigh, ankle, waist. Let them measure and record their own, and then ask someone else to guess which measure belongs around which part of them! (SSM4a,b)

AREA

*   Change the activities described above by asking the children to find out how many different areas they can find on their body. They can either cut paper the same size as their handprint, leg outline, foot print, etc. and compare, or make measurements in square centimetres and compare numbers.

     Extend to asking them to find the surface area of different parts of their body by wrapping paper round bits of them, e.g. arm, torso, leg, foot, and finding the area of the paper. Let them measure and record their own, and then ask someone else to guess which measure belongs around which part of them!

     Can they use the information they have to work out the area of their skin? A close estimate will do! (SSM4a,b)

ACTIVITY 8 # ELASTIC BANDS

┌─────────────── LEARNING OBJECTIVES ───────────────┐

1   Choosing appropriate units of capacity and making
    sensible estimates with them in everyday situations.
2   Extending understanding of the relationship between units.
3   Converting one metric unit to another.
4   Choosing and using appropriate measuring instruments.
5   Interpreting numbers and reading scales to an increasing
    level of accuracy.
6   Developing mathematical strategies and looking for ways
    to overcome difficulties.

└──┘

What you will need

The children will need a variety of containers which will hold more
than 500 millilitres, and some large elastic bands.

What to do

Ask a group of children to:

*   choose a container;
*   place an elastic band round their container to mark where they
    think 500 millilitres of liquid will reach;
*   pour in 500 millilitres of liquid to see how close they were.

The person whose liquid measures the closest to their elastic band
wins the round. They could use one colour of elastic band for the
estimates and another for the actual measure. There will probably
be some discussion about who is the closest and how to check.
Children may just choose to check by eye or to add or take out
liquid until the level exactly matches the elastic band and compare
differences. However, this is often a very difficult idea for the
children to get to grips with.

Organisation

This activity really needs to be supervised for the children to get the
most out of the discussion, while the rest of the class are engaged in
one of the activities at the end of the section or another activity that
the children can work at reasonably independently.

Activities that some children might need to do first

1   Use a clear container. Fill it to an elastic band. Add a plasticine ball and mark the new level. Try different sized plasticine balls. (SSM4a,b)

2   You need:
    • three different containers;
    • one larger, clear container;
    • elastic bands or a waterproof marker;
    • sand or water.
    Fill the three containers. Mark on the large container where you think the water or sand will reach when it is transferred. Try it and see how close you were. (SSM4a)

3   *Fill a pot.*

Reinforcing activities that some children might need

1   *Fill a litre.*

2   Use the same activity as described above, but expecting the children to estimate different amounts of liquid. (SSM4a)

3   *Sponges.*

Activities that some children might be ready to move on to

1   Extend the game by allowing children a second chance, by adjusting their amount of liquid by adding or removing liquid. (SSM4a)

2   *200 grams of plasticine.*

Similar activities for other measures

LENGTH
• The children will need a long piece of string each. Ask them to tie a knot at the place which they think is 50 centimetres from one end. The person who is closest wins the round. Try different lengths for each round. (SSM4a,b)
• *Metre mouse*
• *How high?*

AREA
• *Make a square metre*

MASS
• The children will need access to a selection of objects of different weights. Ask them to make a collection of objects which together they think will weigh 500 grams. Let them check. The person who is closest wins the round. Try different weights for each round. (SSM4a,b)

- *Weigh yourself*
- *Popcorn*
- *How many stones?*

TIME
- Ask a group of children to stand. Let one child use a timer, or watch the clock, and say 'Go' as they start to time one minute. The rest of the group should sit when they think one minute has passed. The person who is closest wins the round. Try different lengths of time for each round, e.g. thirty seconds, fifteen seconds, one-and-a-half minutes, etc. (SSM4a,b)

ANGLE
- The children will need to use paper circles for this game. Ask them to cut out a slice of the circle which they think has an angle of 60°. The person who is closest wins the round. Try different angles for each round. (SSM3c)

ACTIVITY 9 FILL A LITRE

LEARNING OBJECTIVES

1 Choosing appropriate units of capacity and making sensible estimates with them in everyday situations.
2 Extending understanding of the relationship between units. Converting one metric unit to another.
3 Choosing and using appropriate measuring instruments.
4 Interpreting numbers and reading scales to an increasing level of accuracy.
5 Developing mathematical strategies and looking for ways to overcome difficulties.

What you will need
The children will need:

- a container which holds 1 litre;
- a collection of pots which will hold a range of amounts of liquid.

What to do

Ask the children to make a collection of pots which together will fill the litre container exactly. The children may encounter difficulty as they get 'near the top' in the litre container, if they cannot find a single container to complete the litre. They sometimes need encouragement to exchange one of the containers they chose earlier for a different one!

Discuss the collections they have made:

- Who used the most containers?
- Who used the fewest?
- Are there two people who used exactly the same number of containers? Were their collections similar?
- Did the person who used the largest container use the fewest?

FIGURE 33 *Recording*

Ask the children to make a record of the containers they used. Expect them to make a record so that other children may take their work and replicate the collection. The children usually choose to make a written or a pictorial record (see figure 33).

Organisation

This activity works well in one of two ways:

- As a group activity, with the children either working on their own to make their collections or in pairs. Once they have been introduced to the activity, they do not usually need much teacher input (other than passing by with words of encouragement) until they have completed the task, when it is appropriate to discuss their findings with them, either before or after they have made a record of their collections.
- As a task for children to tackle in twos or threes while the rest of the class is engaged in an activity which allows the teacher to creep off to chat to this small group for a few minutes now and then.

Activities that some children might need to do first

1 *Fill a pot.*

2 Sort containers into those which hold more or less than a litre or half a litre. Record the results on a Carroll, Venn or tree diagram. (SSM4a)

Reinforcing activities that some children might need

1 Turn the problem round by asking the children to fill a litre container. Then ask them to make a collection of pots which they think will use up all the water and test to see how close they were. (SSM4a)

2 *Elastic bands.*

3 *Sponges.*

Activities that some children might be ready to move on to

1 Once the children have made their collection, ask them to find out how much liquid each of their small pots will hold. Let them find the total number of millilitres in all their small pots. (It is unlikely that it will be exactly 1000 millilitres, but it will be somewhere close. This inaccuracy of the measurement is worthy of discussion. Why does it happen? Can we make our measurements any more accurate?)

2 *200 grams of plasticine.*

3 *Blanket box.*

4 Try one of these challenges: (SSM4a)
   - Find seven pots which will fill the litre container.
   - Use five pots the same to fill the litre container.
   - Use one large pot and some small ones to fill the litre container.
   - Use six different pots to fill the litre container.
   - Use as many pots as you can to fill the litre container.

Similar activities for other measures

LENGTH

- Use a collection of strips of card, ribbon or string, and a metre stick and set a similar challenge. Ask the children to make a collection of 'lengths' which together will fit alongside the metre stick exactly. The children may encounter difficulty as they get 'near the end' of the metre stick if they cannot find a single strip to complete the metre. They sometimes need encouragement to exchange one of the strips they chose earlier for a different one!

   Discuss the collections they have made;
   - Who used the most strips?
   - Who used the fewest?
   - Are there two people who used exactly the same number of strips? Were their collections similar?
   - Did the person who used the longest strip use the fewest?
- *Metre mouse*
- *How high?*
- *How long?*
- *Ten*
- *Make a line*

AREA

- Use a collection of old cards, postcards, envelopes, tea cards, etc. and a square metre (or a sheet of newspaper or a sheet of A4 paper) and set a similar challenge. Ask the children to make a collection of pictures which together will fit inside the square metre exactly. The children may encounter difficulty as they get near the end of the square metre if they cannot find a single object to complete the metre. They sometimes need encouragement to exchange one of the pictures they chose earlier for a different one!

   Discuss the collections they have made:
   - Who used the most pictures?
   - Who used the fewest?
   - Are there two people who used exactly the same number of pictures? Were their collections similar?
   - Did the person who used the largest pictures use the fewest? (SSM4a)
- *Make a square metre*

MASS

- *Weigh yourself*
- *Popcorn*
- *How many stones?*
- *Gravel balance*

ACTIVITY 10 200 GRAMS OF PLASTICINE

┌─────────────── LEARNING OBJECTIVES ───────────────┐
│   │
│ 1   Understanding and using the language of comparatives. │
│ 2   Understanding and using the language of measures. │
│ 3   Asking questions including 'What would happen if...?' and │
│   'Why?'   │
│   │
└──┘

What you will need

The children will need 200 grams of plasticine each.

What to do

Ask each child to make a different model. Discuss their different attributes, and sort them if appropriate.

*   Which are tall?
*   Which are fat?
*   Which are thin?
*   Which look small?

Put the models on a balance in turn.

*   Do they still weigh the same as when they started?
*   Do they weigh the same as each other?
*   Does it still fit on the balance?

Can they decide on a new model they are planning to make and then make it?

Organisation

The discussion about the models is the most important part of this activity; consequently, the teacher needs to work with a group.

The rest of the class will need to be engaged in one of the activities at the end of the section or some other activity which requires little attention from the teacher.

Activities that some children might need to do first

1   Make a model with plasticine. Find something which balances with it on a pan balance. Change the model without adding more plasticine or taking any off. Does it still balance with the same thing? For example, make a snake and balance it with three pencils. Change it into Humpty Dumpty; does it still balance with the pencils? (SSM4a)

2   *Cones.*

Reinforcing activities that some children might need

1   Try a similar activity to the one described above, but give each of the children in a group ten interlocking cubes to make a model with. Do the models balance? (SSM4a)

2   Use 200 grams of plasticine to make a pot to hold as much liquid as possible. What is the best shape? (SSM4a)

3   *Elastic bands.*

Activities that some children might be ready to move on to

1   Use clay, and let a group of children make some pots. When they are dry, ask the children to find out which holds the most sand. Can they put the pots in order according to how much they will hold? (SSM4a)

2   Let the children use plasticine to make a collection of capacity measures. (SSM4a)

Similar activities for other measures

LENGTH
*   Give each of the children in a group a 1 metre strip of paper. Let them cut it up and stick it on a bright piece of paper to make a picture. Are all the pictures the same? (SSM4a)
*   *Metre mouse*
*   *How long?*

AREA
*   Let all the children in a group have half a sheet of A4 paper. Let them cut it up and stick it down on a bright piece of paper to make a picture. They must use all the paper. Are all the pictures the same? (SSM4a)
*   *Make a square metre*

MASS
*   *Weigh yourself*
*   *Popcorn*
*   *How many stones?*
*   *Gravel balance*

ACTIVITY 11 GUESS WHICH BOX

┌─────────────── LEARNING OBJECTIVES ───────────────┐
1 Trying different mathematical approaches.
2 Identifying and obtaining information needed to carry out the work.
3 Finding volumes by counting methods.
4 Finding areas by counting methods.
└──┘

What you will need

The children will need a collection of boxes and access to a variety of measuring implements.

In preparation for the activity, the teacher will need to have chosen one of the boxes and found out the answers to the following questions about it:

- How tall is the box?
- How wide is the box?
- How deep is the box?
- How many cubes does it hold?
- How many sheets of A4 would you need to cover it?

This information needs to be made available to the children. Teachers may like to use the clue worksheet on page 119.

What to do

Ask the children to be 'box detectives' and use the clues to help them find the box that was chosen.

Organisation

Most children can be left with a reasonably free rein to tackle this activity. They seem to work best in groups of two or three. They may need encouragement to keep track of their findings in some way!

Activities that some children might need to do first

1 *Floor plans.*

2 Fill boxes with cubes and count. Fill them so that you can fit as many as possible in each (by packing them neatly) and as few as possible (by flinging them in haphazardly). (SSM4c)

3 *Junk boxes.*

Reinforcing activities that some children might need

1   Let the children write their own clues to describe a box, i.e. it holds fifty-seven conkers, you need one and a half sheets of A4 to cover it, its dimensions are 25 centimetres x 10 centimetres x 38 centimetres. (SSM4c)

Activities that some children might be ready to move on to

1   Measure the height, width and depth of several boxes in cubes. Fill them with cubes. Make a table to record results. Can you predict? (SSM4c)

ACTIVITY 12 CONES

```
LEARNING OBJECTIVES

1   Making three-dimensional shapes with an increasing
    degree of accuracy.
2   Finding volumes by counting methods.
3   Developing mathematical strategies and looking for ways
    to overcome difficulties.
```

What you will need

The children will need:

- thin card;
- scissors;
- pencils;
- something to draw a circle with (compasses or plates to draw round);
- some clean, safe, empty cans;
- some sand or stones.

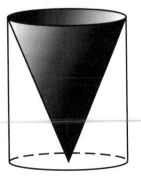

What to do

Teachers need to be aware that there is a relationship between a cone and a cylinder with the same height and the same radius. The volume of the cone is one third the volume of the cylinder.

Remind the children how to make a cone from part of a circle. Let them choose a can, and try to make a cone to fit inside the can exactly, i.e. it needs to be the same height as the can, and the circumference of the finished cone needs to fit snugly inside the open top of the can (see figure 34).

FIGURE 34 *A cone inside a can*

Children will often need several attempts at this and they need to be encouraged to think of the two dimensions mentioned above – height and circumference – and to relate those to the large circle that they are making their cone from. The teacher will need to guide the children with questions like:

- How will you make the cone taller?
- Will you need to start with the same-sized circle next time?
- Is half a circle about the right size to start with or do you really need more/less?

Organisation

Provided there are sufficient cans available, this activity can work well as a class activity, or as one which most of the children can be involved in while others are engaged in something which requires more input from the teacher. This activity does, however, require the teacher to 'pass by' with encouraging words and suggestions occasionally, so that children persist with it in a meaningful way, and learn from any mistakes they are making.

Activities that some children might need to do first

1   Make cone hats. (SSM2b)

2   Make 'ice-cream cones' with cotton wool or ping-pong balls as ice-cream. (SSM2b)

Reinforcing activities that some children might need

1   Ask a group of children to make a collection of different-sized cones and order them by how much sand/stones/cubes they will hold. (SSM2b,4c)

Activities that some children might be ready to move on to

1   Extend the original activity by asking the children to fill the cone they have made with sand or stones, and find out how many 'conefuls' will fill their can. (It should be about three!) Is this always the case? (SSM2b, 4c)

2   Make a pyramid to fit inside a box. Let the children select a box, and use thin card or thick paper to build a pyramid that will fit inside their box exactly (see figure 35). This is difficult! Children may also wish to go on and make the same comparisons as described in 1. (The answer should be about the same!) (SSM2b)

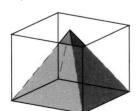

FIGURE 35 *A pyramid inside a box*

Similar activities for other measures

LENGTH
- *Sorting box*
- *How long?*
- *Plasticine sausages*

TIME
- *How long?*
- *Plasticine models*

WEIGHT
- *Magnets*

ACTIVITY 13   FLOOR PLANS

LEARNING OBJECTIVES

---

1   Finding volumes by counting methods.
2   Developing mathematical strategies and looking for ways of overcoming difficulties.

What you will need

The children will need plenty of interlocking cubes and some 'floor plans' (see worksheet on page 120). (Children will need a copy of this sheet which has been cut into separate plans.) Teachers may choose to make up some more plans of their own.

What to do

Ask the children to choose a floor plan. The plan shows the dimensions of a building. The children need to take how many cubes they think they will need and build a building which will stand on their plan.

Can they make three or four different buildings, each of which can stand on the same plan?

Organisation

Children work well in a group on this activity. Teachers may wish to make it more meaningful for them by drawing a simple road system on a large piece of paper, and asking the children to work with one floor plan between two to make buildings to stand alongside the road, and therefore turn it into a town.

The activity itself requires little teacher input, other than to 'pass by' occasionally, and encourage the children to make a variety of different buildings. Because children can largely get on with this activity, teachers may feel that it is appropriate to have several groups working on these buildings (if there are enough cubes available!) and support some children by discussing what they have made and, as they are ready, to move them on to some of the reinforcement or extension ideas.

Activities that some children might need to do first

1   How many different buildings can you make with four cubes? Five cubes? Six cubes? (SSM4c)

2   Use the cubes or Lego to make homes for plasticine models of animals. (SSM4a)

3   Discuss different types of building, especially blocks of flats. Use the cubes or Lego to make some. (SSM4a)

Reinforcing activities that some children might need

1   Play 'Buildings'. Each child aims to make a building out of cubes to agreed dimensions, e.g. 3 x 4 x 6. They take it in turns to grab one handful of cubes and build. The first person to finish their building with no spares wins the game. (SSM4a,c)

2   Take twenty-four cubes. How many different buildings can you make? The children will need to agree on whether buildings must be cuboids or whether they can have more adventurous shapes. (SSM4c)

Activities that some children might be ready to move on to

1   Take one floor plan, e.g. 2 x 3. Build a one-storey building. How many cubes? Build a two-storey building. How many?, etc. Is there a pattern? Try other floor plans. (SSM4c)

CAPACITY/VOLUME ACTIVITIES FOR THE REST OF THE CLASS

These ideas are designed for children to use with little support from the teacher, other than initial clarification. Teachers may choose to turn them into worksheets or challenge cards, or simply to explain to the children what is expected of them. Some activities are appropriate for a group to work on, others can be used with a whole class.

1   Use a water trough and a collection of containers. Fill them all to the top. (SSM4a)

2   Use a water trough and a collection of containers. Mark a level on the containers with an elastic band. Pour water in to that level. (SSM4a)

3   Use a water trough and a collection of containers. Sort them into those which hold more/less than a yoghurt pot. (SSM4a)

4   Use a water trough and a collection of containers. Find pairs of containers which hold the same. (SSM4a)

5   Choose ten containers. Choose a small pot or carton as a unit of measure. Find out and record how many potfuls fill each. Order them accordingly. (SSM4a,c)

6   Fill boxes with cubes. Choose some containers. Find out and record how many cubes fill each. Order them accordingly. (SSM4a)

7   Use cubes and some containers. Find six containers that you can fill with between twenty and thirty cubes. (SSM4a,c)

8   Use base ten blocks. Take blocks to the total value of 234. These need not necessarily be taken as two hundreds, three tens and four ones.) Make a model with the blocks. Make two more worth the same. (SSM4a,c)

9   Make a collection of boxes which together will hold a cubic metre of sand. (SSM4a,c)

10 Measure out 200 millilitres of orange juice into paper cups for everyone in the class. (SSM4a,b)

11 Order a collection of vegetables according to how much space they take up. (SSM4a)

12 Use a litre container, and a collection of smaller containers:
    • find seven pots which will fill it;
    • find five pots the same to fill it;
    • find one large pot and some small ones to fill it;
    • find six different pots to fill it;
    • use as many pots as you can to fill it. (SSM4a)

FIGURE 36 *Worksheet 12* – Guess which box

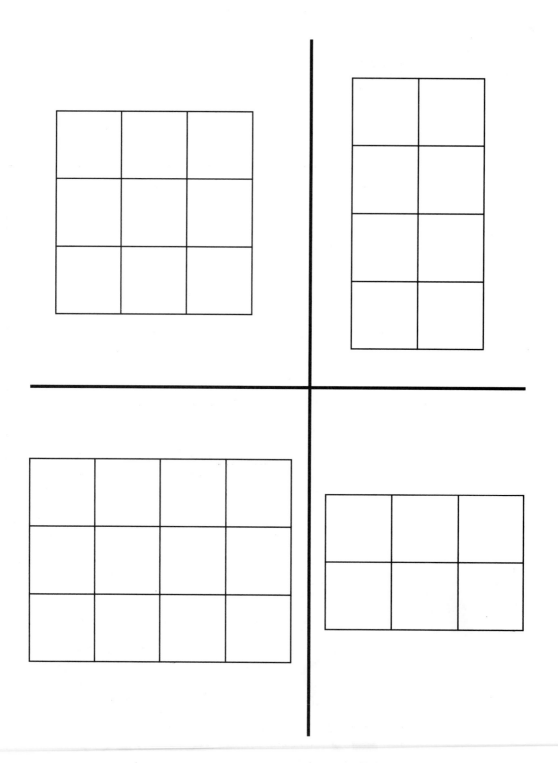

FIGURE 37 *Worksheet 13* – Floor plans
Hodder & Stoughton © 1996 Janine Blinko and Ann Slater Teaching Measures. The publishers grant permission for multiple copies of this worksheet to be made in the place of purchase for use solely in that institution.

CHAPTER

TIME

This chapter includes:

- Introduction
- Clock patience
- Take your time
- Modelling
- Busy times
- Time lines
- Days of the week
- A big clock
- Jar lids
- How long did it take?
- Digital display
- Time activities for the rest of the class

The problems related to this section are:

- How much do you drink in a day?   (page 188)
- Invent a new way of measuring   (page 194)
- Plan a trip   (page 196)
- Plan a picnic   (page 196)
- Plan a bring-and-buy sale   (page 197)
- Make a clock   (page 198)

INTRODUCTION

Time is a difficult measure in that it is not something that you can see or touch. The use of an analogue clock helps to support the notion of the cyclical nature of time, but there are other ideas that children need to be helped with. They need to understand that:

- a period of time has a start and an end point;
- events can be sequenced in time;
- speed is different from time.

The National Curriculum suggests certain goals at each Key Stage in the understanding of the measurement of time (see figure 38).

	Pupils should be taught to:
Key Stage 1	**a** compare events using appropriate language, by direct comparison; begin to use standard units of time, choosing units appropriate to a situation; estimate with these units
	b choose and use simple measuring instruments, reading and interpreting numbers and scales with some accuracy
Key Stage 2	**a** choose appropriate standard units of time and make sensible estimates with them in everyday situations; extend their understanding of the relationship between units
	b choose and use the appropriate measuring instruments; interpret numbers and read scales to an increasing degree of accuracy

FIGURE 38 *Key Stage goals – Time*

ACTIVITY I   CLOCK PATIENCE

┌─────────────── LEARNING OBJECTIVES ───────────────┐

1   Reading and interpreting numbers with increasing
    accuracy.
2   Organising and checking work.

└──┘

What you will need

The children will need to use an ordinary pack of playing cards or a set of number cards with four each of the numbers one to twelve and four blank cards.

What to do

This is a traditional card game which some children may already be familiar with. If an ordinary pack of playing cards is being used, children will need to be able to accept that a Jack represents eleven, a Queen represents twelve and the King belongs in the middle of the clock.

PREPARATION
The cards need to be shuffled and dealt out as if they were the numbers on a clock, plus the centre (see figure 39). (There will be four cards in each pile.)

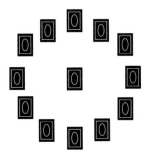

FIGURE 39 *Clock patience*

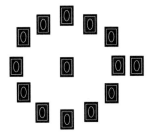

FIGURE 40 *Playing Clock patience*

PLAYING THE GAME

This is a game for children to play on their own or in pairs. The top card in the middle is turned over. It must then be placed wherever it belongs on the clock. For example, if a three is turned, it must be placed where three belongs on a clock (see figure 40).

The next card is turned from the three's place. The goal is to end up with all the cards in the 'right' places. This is not easy – sometimes the last card from a pile is already in the right pile and play is stopped before all the other piles have been used up. For example, if the last card to be turned in the three's place is a three, there is no move to instigate turning a card from another pile! The aim of the game is to have all the cards in the right places.

Organisation

It is possible to introduce this game to the whole class, but there may be a lot of questions the first time the children play, so it seems to work better if a group of children are introduced to the game, and they are then responsible for teaching others. (Teachers may wish to 'hand pick' the first group.) While the group(s) are playing, the rest of the class can be engaged in one of the activities on page 140.

Activities that some children might need to do first

1 Make clocks from paper plates. (SSM4a)

2 Make a collection of pictures of clocks from old magazines and make a collage with them, or sort them on Venn, Carroll or tree diagrams. (SSM4a)

Reinforcing activities that some children might need

1 *A big clock.*

2 Hide the classroom clock and ask the children to draw a picture of it. (SSM4a)

3 Ask the children to make their own clock puzzle:
   • draw a clock face;
   • cut it into at least six 'sensible' pieces;
   • ask a friend to remake the clock! (SSM4a)

Activities that some children might be ready to move on to

1 Make a clock face with junk boxes. (SSM4a)

2 Extend activity 1 to make a clock which works. (SSM4a)

3 Try the above activities but using a digital clock as the aim. (SSM4a)

4 *Digital display.*

5 *How long does it take?*

ACTIVITY 2   TAKE YOUR TIME

─────────────── LEARNING OBJECTIVES ───────────────

1   Comparing events using appropriate language by direct
     comparison.
2   Understanding and using the language of comparatives.

What you will need

The children will need:

- a collection of old magazines, comics, newspapers and other
  pictures;
- scissors;
- paper and glue;
- task cards made from the worksheet on page 142.

What to do

Give individual children (or pairs or groups of children) one of the
task cards. Ask them to collect pictures of things as indicated on
their card. For example, if they choose the card which says 'Things
which take a long time to happen', they may cut out and stick a
picture of a flower, because a plant may seem to take a long time to
grow to the children.

   This activity is particularly interesting if similar pictures appear
on more than one sheet. For example, a flower may also appear on
the 'happen quickly' sheet because, compared to the time a child
takes to grow, a flower does not grow quickly. This comparative
discussion is essential.

Organisation

This activity can be organised in a number of ways. Once initiated, it
only requires that the teacher 'pass by' occasionally to help
discussion along.

- Children can work in pairs with one or all of the task cards. If
  they use more than one card, they will need a sheet of paper for
  each group, and they will need to keep themselves organised.
- A group of six can work with a large sheet of paper for sticking
  on and one task card. If children are working in this way, the
  whole class can be engaged in the same activity but using
  different task cards. All the results can then be displayed,
  compared and discussed.

- Individual children can work with one or more task card. If they have more than three cards, they often get in a muddle or lose interest.

Activities that some children might need to do first

1 *Plasticine models.*

Reinforcing activities that some children might need

1 Ask the children to make a list of some of the things they have done in a day, e.g. eating breakfast, writing a story, coming to school. Let them draw a picture of each one. Can they peg the pictures in order on a washing line (piece of string suspended across the classroom), according to how long they took? The children can tackle this either by estimating or by actually timing themselves doing the different things. (SSM4a)

Activities that some children might be ready to move on to

1 *Jar lids.*

2 Ask the children to produce a breakdown of different people's days: how much time is spent eating, working, sleeping, watching TV, exercising, playing, etc.? (SSM4a)

3 *Time lines.*

Similar activities for other measures

LENGTH
- *Sorting box*
- *How long?*
- *Plasticine sausages*
- *Bodies*
- *Detectives*
- *Make a line*

AREA
- *Shadows*
- *Boxes*
- *Letter shapes*
- *Cones*

WEIGHT
- *Plasticine models*

ACTIVITY 3   MODELLING

┌─────────────── LEARNING OBJECTIVES ───────────────┐

1   Comparing events using appropriate language by direct comparison.

2   Understanding the language of comparatives.

└──┘

What you will need

The children will need plasticine, or some other type of modelling clay, and a surface to work on.

What to do

Ask the children to think of a model that they are going to make, e.g. a plasticine mouse. Ask them to take a long time making it.

Then ask them to make another one, but to make one very quickly. Compare and discuss the outcomes with them.

- Are the ones which took more time better?
- Why?
- Is it always true that the longer something takes to make, the better it is?

Organisation

This works well as both a group and class activity. The discussion about whether or not rushed work is best, and whether or not work which is done extremely slowly is best, clearly has implications for other work the children are involved with. This is an effective way of illustrating something that teachers may frequently say to children.

If the actual 'timing' is only done with a group, the rest of the class can either make a plasticine model of their own or be involved in the activity offered in *How long?*

Activities that some children might need to do first

1   Discuss who gets ready the quickest for playtime or PE. (SSM4a)

2   Ask the children to write their names quickly and then slowly. Discuss the outcomes. (SSM4a)

3   *How long?*

Reinforcing activities that some children might need

1   Compare three or four children making different plasticine models. Order the models by the length of time they took to make. This can be done either by comparison or by asking the children to time their model-making on the clock or on a stopwatch. (SSM4a)

2   Let the children design a list of activities. Ask them to order them according to how long they take, e.g. do up my coat, walk around the school. Compare two children's results – why might they differ? (SSM4a)

Activities that some children might be ready to move on to

1   Extend the idea by asking the children to make a variety of models and sort them onto Carroll, Venn and tree diagrams, e.g. takes as long as, longer than a cat to make. Extend the idea further by bringing in standard time, e.g. takes less than two minutes to make. (SSM4a)

2   *Jar lids.*

3   *A big clock.*

ACTIVITY 4   BUSY TIMES

┌─────────────── LEARNING OBJECTIVES ───────────────┐

    1   Comparing events using appropriate language by direct
         comparison.
    2   Understanding the language of comparatives.

└──┘

What you will need

The children will need access to pictures of a variety of environments, such as a greengrocer's shop, a bank, a classroom, a home, a garden, a park, a playground, etc. These pictures can be ones that the children have drawn themselves or collected from magazines, or photographs. They will also need a copy of the worksheet on page 143.

What to do

Ask the children to choose one place to think about. Give them some research time, maybe overnight, or a discussion time with other children who have chosen the same picture. Ask them to decide which would be the busiest time in each of those places.

The worksheet is blank to enable children to use it for their responses to a variety of questions. The children may need to write words, draw pictures or draw clocks to answer one or all of the following:

- What is the busiest time of year?
- What is the busiest time of the week?
- What is the busiest time of day?
- When might this place be empty?
- When might it be quiet?
- When might it be dark?
- Why?

Organisation

This activity works well as a class activity, particularly if the children are co-operating well with one or two others who are considering the same place.

Activities that some children might need to do first

1   Use a picture of an empty classroom (for example) and stamp or draw a clock on it, with a time indicated. Ask the children to draw what might be going on in that place at that time. What might have happened just before? Just after? (SSM4a)

2   Ask the children to order events of their day, i.e. drawing or using pictures of getting up, having breakfast, going to school, playing, going home, having tea and going to bed, and placing them in order. (SSM4a)

3   Similarly, events during the year can be ordered: leaves growing, summer break from school, etc. (SSM4a)

Reinforcing activities that some children might need

1   Let the children work in pairs to study different parts of the school – when are the busiest/quietest times? Does it differ for different parts of the school? (SSM4a)

2   Interview different people around the school: caretaker, lollipop lady, secretary, teacher, children, head. When are the busiest times of day for them? What about the children's families? (SSM4a)

Activities that some children might be ready to move on to

1   Identify a place in or within sight of the school and record how busy it is at regular intervals during the day, either by counting the number of people or by categorising (very busy, busy, quite busy, not very busy, quiet, empty) and making a pictorial representation of the results. It is interesting to compare results between places and try to explain why they occur. (SSM4a)

2   *Days of the week.*

ACTIVITY 5   TIME LINES

┌─────── LEARNING OBJECTIVES ───────┐

1   Comparing events using appropriate language by direct comparison.
2   Using standard units of time.
3   Discussing work.
4   Responding to and asking mathematical questions.

What you will need

The children will need:

- a long piece of string or an old washing line strung across the class at a height they can reach;
- some pegs;
- paper and pens;
- maybe some labels with the names of the months on them.

What to do

The children may need to do some research at home in advance of the opening discussion for this activity. Discuss with the children things which have happened in the past year in their lives, in the lives of their families, in the life of the school, in nature, in their town, in the country, in the world. (December or January are good times for this, when the Sunday papers do their 'review of the year'.)

Ask every child to make a record of one event on paper by any method they choose, i.e. drawing, painting, cutting and sticking pictures from papers, writing. The pictures can then be pegged on the line in the order that they happened. The children may find it helpful to have month labels on the line already.

Discuss the outcomes with the children and let them comment on the results:

- Do you remember it being summer when your mum got a new car?
- Which was the quietest season for news?
- Do you think that any of these things will happen at the same time next year?
- Do you think June was a good time to have the school painted?
- What would be the best time?

Organisation

This activity works well as a class activity. It seems to be necessary to give the children a time limit to complete their pictures, otherwise the speedy ones have a long wait for those who are enjoying making elaborate pictures. Alternatively, the post mortem discussion can be postponed until later in the same day.

Activities that some children might need to do first

1   A similar activity, but ordering events in a day, week, month or term. (SSM4a)

2   Use seeds and vegetables. Time, chart and compare their growth in a variety of ways, e.g. which grow most quickly? Draw pictures of the stages of development at regular intervals. Muddle up the pictures and ask the children to re-order them. (SSM4a)

3   Extension activities from *Days of the week*.

Reinforcing activities that some children might need

1   Compare the growth of different plants/seeds on a year's time line and on a term's time line. When do they grow best? How do they grow? Do some take longer to germinate? Do some grow quicker than others? Why might that be? (SSM4a)

2   Let two or three children co-operate to produce a year's time line which illustrates the important events that have happened in their lives. (SSM4a)

3   Chart the moon each night over an extended period of time and collect information; record it on a calendar or a number line. Ask the children to look for a pattern. (SSM4a)

Activities that some children might be ready to move on to

1   Make time lines which cover a lifetime (either their own, or a famous person).
      Make a time line to illustrate important events in the history of the school.
      Make a time line to illustrate significant events in the last century.
      It is interesting to spend time with the children comparing the outcomes of these different time lines. Things which are important at a personal level in the past year cannot be compared with significant events in a century, such as the comparison between getting a new swing for a birthday and the first man on the moon. Children usually have a surprisingly sensible perception of these things. (SSM4a)

2   *Busy times.*

3   *Days of the week.*

Similar activities for other measures

LENGTH
- *Bodies*
- *Detectives*
- *Make a line*

AREA
- *Shadows*
- *Boxes*
- *Letter shapes*

WEIGHT
- *Plasticine models*

ACTIVITY 6   DAYS OF THE WEEK

┌─────────────── LEARNING OBJECTIVES ───────────────┐

1   Comparing events using appropriate language by direct comparison.
2   Understanding the language of comparatives.

└──┘

What you will need

The children will need three sets of 'days of the week' cards made from the worksheet on page 144.

What to do

This game is appropriate for a group of two or three children. If you wish to play with a larger group, you will need more sets of cards.

The cards need to be shuffled, placed upside down and spread out between all the players. The children take it in turns to pick up one card. The aim of the game is for the children to collect one of each of the days of the week and to place them in order. If they do not need the card they pick up, it is replaced and they must wait for their next turn. This game can also be played using a set of month cards or season cards.

Organisation

The children will need to play the game under the supervision of the teacher, another adult or a child who can read, to help them with the words. Alternatively, teachers may feel that it is appropriate to add picture clues to the cards, e.g. a seasonal tree on the seasons. Once they have played a few times, the initial sounds give them clues, and between the children in the group they can usually (!) decipher all the words; then the teacher need only 'pass by' occasionally as they play.

As the teacher works with the group, the rest of the class can be engaged in one of the activities at the end of this section which need little supervision.

Activities that some children might need to do first

1 Recite the days of the week. (SSM4a)

2 Initial sounds activities.

3 Discussions about days of the week; today, yesterday, before and after and next. (SSM4a)

4 Daily calendars or weather charts. (SSM4a)

Reinforcing activities that some children might need

1 Identification of things that happen on particular days, e.g. We have PE on Wednesdays. (SSM4a)

2 Use the *Days of the week* worksheet on page 144. Rather than cutting along the black lines as shown, cut wiggly lines, and turn the sheet into a jigsaw puzzle for the children to make. (SSM4a)

Activities that some children might be ready to move on to

1   Play the same game, using cards made from months or seasons sheets instead. (SSM4a)

ACTIVITY 7   A BIG CLOCK

┌─────────────────── LEARNING OBJECTIVES ───────────────────┐

1   Using standard units of time.
2   Choosing and using simple measuring instruments.
3   Reading and interpreting numbers and scales with some accuracy.
4   Selecting and using the appropriate mathematics and materials.

└───┘

What you will need

The children will need two skipping ropes of different lengths, a set of large number cards (one to twelve) and a space.

What to do

Twelve children need to be chosen to hold the numbers. One child needs to be chosen to hold one end of both ropes. Two other children need to be chosen to hold the other ends.

Set the rest of the children the task of directing the 'holders' so that they make a large clock face on the floor, using the numbers, and the ropes as hands (see figure 41).

When they have made the clock, it can be used to play a number of games, where the 'holders' play against the others.

* The two teams take it in turns.
* The others ask the holders to show a time, e.g. half past three. If the holders show the correct time, they score a point.
* The holders make a time and the others have to read the time correctly. If they are correct, they score a point.
* The winning team has the most points after eight rounds.

Children may need to help each other by making the correct times on a clock face first. Teachers may choose to limit the times the children can use for this game, i.e. just o'clocks or half pasts, or to use some of the cards available on the worksheet on page 145.

FIGURE 41 *A large clock face on the floor*

Organisation

This activity is really only successful if the whole class is involved and there is a large space available to work in. The children really need to have a clock available in the room to look at.

Activities that some children might need to do first

1   Play with old clocks. (SSM4a)

2   Make clocks from paper plates. (SSM4a)

3   Make collections of different clocks from old magazines. (SSM4a)

4   Play the same game as described above using a clock to demonstrate times. The holders must make the same time as shown on the demonstration clock. (SSM4a)

5   *Clock patience.*

Reinforcing activities that some children might need

1   Make a set of work cards with appropriate times on (see page 145). Let children take it in turns or work in pairs to choose a card and direct the hand holders to show the time indicated. (SSM4a)

2   Print a clock with children's hands where the thumb indicates hours and fingers indicate minutes. Make hands which move. Use the clock during the school day to indicate when 'events', e.g. a TV programme, are likely to happen. (SSM4a)

Activities that some children might be ready to move on to

1   This game can be varied by using digital time cards. The others choose a digital time that the holders must show. The holders show a time, and the others must write down the correct digital equivalent. (SSM4a,b)

2   Use the earlier/later cards from page 145 to make small game cards. Let the 'others' get themselves into two teams. The person holding the two ropes chooses a starting time, and the clock is organised to show that time.

  The teams take it in turns to choose a card and change the clock according to the directions on the card. If they are correct, they score a point. The team with the most points after five rounds wins the game.

  This game can be extended so that each team sets an earlier/later challenge for the other. (SSM4a,b)

3   *Digital display.*

ACTIVITY 8   # JAR LIDS

┌─────────────── LEARNING OBJECTIVES ───────────────┐

1   Choosing appropriate standard units of time.
2   Extending understanding of the relationship between units.
3   Choosing and using appropriate measuring instruments.
4   Interpreting numbers and reading scales to an increasing level of accuracy.
5   Checking results and considering whether they are reasonable.

└──┘

What you will need

The children will need:

- a large and varied collection of old jar lids (unless the children are very responsible with sharp objects, the teacher will need to have made one, two or three small holes in each lid);
- access to a sink, tank or bucket with water in;
- a timing device with a second facility, i.e. a clock with a second hand or a stopwatch.

What to do

Let the children choose four or five lids to experiment with. Ask them to place them in the water like boats and to order them according to how long they take to sink.

This challenge can be addressed in a number of different ways:

- by placing them all in the water at the same time and recording the order in which they reach the bottom (it is very tricky to start them all simultaneously);
- by placing them in the water two at a time and ordering them according to the outcomes;
- by placing them in the water one at a time and finding out how many seconds each one takes to sink and ordering them accordingly.

Ask them questions about what they have found out:

- Does the largest lid take the longest to sink?
- Are there two which take the same time to sink?
- What makes a good sinker?

Organisation

Because of the potential 'hazards' of children using water, it is best if only two or three pairs of children work on this activity at any one time. It is also best if each pair has its own water tank.

The rest of the class can be involved in one of the low-teacher input activities, or they could be in making 'tockers', as described in the **Reinforcing activities** section.

Activities that some children might need to do first

1   Time the children doing things – reading a page, writing a page, etc. – or let them time themselves, using a variety of devices, e.g. timers, tockers, stopwatches, clocks, home-made clocks. Discuss the outcomes with them.

Time adults doing things – reading the paper, writing a letter, cooking lunch. Guess and check. (SSM4a,b)

2   As activity 1, above, but let them time each other. (SSM4a,b)

3   *Plasticine models.*

Reinforcing activities that some children might need

1   Make tockers with jar lids.

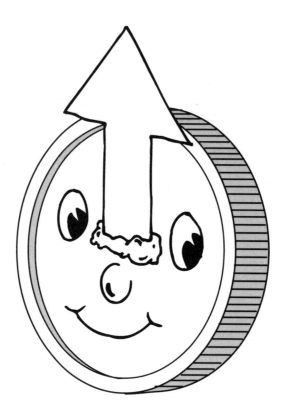

FIGURE 42 *A tocker*

Let the children choose what size lid they use and how much plasticine. Test them to find out whose tocks the longest and quickest. Set challenges about the tockers they have made. What determines how long it tocks for? Is it position or quantity of plasticine, or size of lid, or some other factor? (SSM4a)

2   *How long did it take?*

Activities that some children might be ready to move on to

1   Ask the children to sort the lids onto a Carroll, Venn or tree diagram by a variety of criteria, for example 'Tocks for longer than thirty seconds'. (SSM4a,b)

2   Let the children design a list of activities. Ask them to sort them by those which can and cannot be completed before the tocker stops, e.g. do up my coat, walk around the school. Compare two children's results – why might they differ? (SSM4a)

3   Ask the children to find a variety of objects which sink, and order them, e.g. card, a key, a plastic cube, a bean. (SSM4a)

ACTIVITY 9

HOW LONG DID IT TAKE?

┌─────────── LEARNING OBJECTIVES ───────────┐

1   Choosing appropriate standard units of time.
2   Extending understanding of the relationship between units.
3   Choosing and using appropriate measuring instruments.
4   Interpreting numbers and reading scales to an increasing
     degree of accuracy.
5   Developing mathematical strategies and looking for ways
     to overcome difficulties.

└──┘

What you will need

The children will need:

*   a clock stamp and some paper;
*   workcards made from the worksheets on page 146;
*   sight of the classroom clock.

What to do

Ask the children to:

*   take a piece of paper;
*   print two clock faces on it;
*   choose one of the activity cards.

The children should do the activity indicated on the card, but they should also make a copy of the position of the hands on the classroom clock as they begin the activity and as they finish it.

The children do not necessarily need to be able to tell the time. At one level, it develops the notion of the passage of time, and that the hands are recording that in some way. At another level, the children can be asked one or some of the following questions.

*   Can they tell the times on the clocks?
*   Can they work out how long the activity has taken them?
*   Looking at them again tomorrow, can they tell which activities were tackled in the morning, and which in the afternoon?

Organisation

This activity works well as both a class activity and a group activity.

Activities that some children might need to do first

1   Use their arms to indicate times shown on the clock face. (SSM4a)

2   *Clock patience.*

Reinforcing activities that some children might need

1   *A big clock* and its reinforcing activities.

2   Record starting and finishing times of other classroom activities that they are involved in. (This often motivates some of the less speedy children to hurry along!) (SSM4a,b)

Activities that some children might be ready to move on to

1   Turn the problem around by specifying starting and finishing times for particular activities and expecting the children to achieve the goals set.
   A useful discussion can follow this, where children give their opinions on whether or not they think they were allowed enough or too much time. Similarly, it is enlightening to allow the children to disclose their strategies for keeping to the times allowed. (SSM4a,b)

2   *Digital display.*

ACTIVITY 10   DIGITAL DISPLAY

LEARNING OBJECTIVES
---

1   Choosing appropriate standard units of time.
2   Extending understanding of the relationship between units.
3   Converting one metric unit to another.
4   Interpreting numbers and reading scales to an increasing level of accuracy.
5   Understanding and using the language of measures.

What you will need

The children will need four sets of digital digits (0–9), as found on a digital clock display, and a point card (a card with a colon).

What to do

Four children are chosen as digit holders, and a fifth as a 'point'. Each of the four children has a set of digit cards, and they stand in a line, two either side of the colon. They choose one of the numbers and hold it up for the rest of the class or group to see.

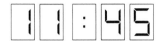

FIGURE 43 *Holding up numbers.*

The rest of the group are sorted into two teams. They take it in turns to read the 'times' displayed. If they read the time correctly, they score a point; if not, they miss a turn.

The group of five children who are displaying the times will need to confer over the times they are making. After ten rounds, the team with the most points wins the game. Talk with them about the game:

- Does everyone need a complete set of digits?
- Do all the times make sense?
- Is there another way to show 15:30? (3:30 p.m.!)

Organisation

This works well as a class game, but teachers may wish to change it into a game that four children can play. In this version of the game, the children need to be in two groups of two. Each pair takes it in turn to make a time for the other team to read.

Activities that some children might need to do first

1 Read digital times. (SSM4b)

2 *A big clock.*

3 *How long did it take?*

Reinforcing activities that some children might need

1 Use straws or matchsticks as light bars on a digital clock display. Set the children challenges like:
- What is the earliest time of day you can make with sixteen light bars?
- How many different times of day can you make with sixteen light bars?
- Find two times of day which use the same number of light bars. (SSM4a,b)

Activities that some children might be ready to move on to

1 Use the time cards suggested in *A big clock* where the times are written in words. Ask the children to 'translate' the times into digital times. (SSM4a,b)

2 Use the earlier/later sheet from *A big clock* on page 145 to make small game cards, and some digital time cards as shown in figure 44. Let a group of children divide themselves into two teams.

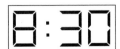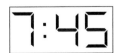

FIGURE 44 *Digital time cards*

The time cards and the 'earlier/later' cards are placed upside down on the table. The teams take it in turns to turn over a time card and an 'earlier/later' card. They are to write down what the digital clock would look like after it had changed according to the earlier/later rule. If they are correct, they keep the cards; if not, they are replaced.

This game can be extended so that each team sets an earlier/later challenge for the other rather than using the cards. (SSM4a,b)

Similar activities for other measures

LENGTH
- *Metre mouse*
- *How high?*

AREA
- *Make a square metre*

CAPACITY/VOLUME
- *Blanket Box*
- *Elastic bands*
- *Fill a litre*
- *200 grams of plasticine*
- *Guess which box*

WEIGHT
- *Weigh yourself*
- *How many stones?*
- *Gravel balance*

TIME ACTIVITIES FOR THE REST OF THE CLASS

These ideas are designed for children to use with little support from the teacher, other than initial clarification. Teachers may choose to turn them into worksheets or challenge cards, or simply to explain to the children what is expected of them. Some activities are appropriate for a group to work on, others can be used with a whole class.

1   Put each of the following challenges on a workcard of its own: Use plasticine to respond to the challenge. Choose the right timer and record each result. (SSM4a,b)
- How many letters can you make in three minutes?
- Can you make your name in less than five minutes?
- Can you make a sausage 50 cm long in one minute?
- Make a bowl of plasticine fruit in ten minutes.
- How many plasticine balls can you make in thirty seconds?

2   Use a TV guide or a class timetable as a reference. Copy the times and the titles of some programmes you would like to watch. (SSM4a)

3   Use the *Today, yesterday and tomorrow* sheet on page 147. Finish the sentences. Draw pictures to match. (SSM4a)

4   Use one sheet of paper for each day of the week. Write the day, and draw and/or write about one thing you usually do on that day. (SSM4a)

5   Use the *Appointments* worksheet on page 148. Use the schedule to make out appointment cards for each of the patients. (SSM4a)

Things which take a long time to happen.

Things which happen quickly.

Things which start at a particular time.

Different types of clock.

Things which take about the same time as travelling to your friend's house.

Things which take about the same time as watching your favourite TV programme.

Things which take about the same time as getting to school.

FIGURE 45 *Worksheet 14 – Take your time*

Busy times

Quiet times

Empty times

Monday

Tuesday

Wednesday

Thursday

Friday

Saturday

Sunday

FIGURE 47 *Worksheet 16 – Days of the week*

one o'clock	two hours later
15 minutes later	4:45
45 minutes earlier	seven o'clock
half past four	1 ½ hours later
half an hour earlier	half past ten
five minutes earlier	12:15

FIGURE 48 *Worksheet 17 – A big clock*
Hodder & Stoughton © 1996 Janine Blinko and Ann Slater Teaching Measures. The publishers grant permission for multiple copies of this worksheet to be made in the place of purchase for use solely in that institution.

Draw a picture of everyone in your family.	Pick up all the rubbish outside the school building.
Write your name 100 times.	Sing all the nursery rhymes you can think of.
Tidy the books.	Ask your teacher what you can do to help.
Walk around the school ten times.	Draw what you see out of the window.
Write all the numbers to 100.	Make a boat out of paper.

FIGURE 49 *Worksheet 18 – How long did it take?*
Hodder & Stoughton © 1996 Janine Blinko and Ann Slater Teaching Measures. The publishers grant permission for multiple copies of this worksheet to be made in the place of purchase for use solely in that institution.

Today is ....
On .... we usually ....
....

Yesterday was ....
On .... we usually ....
....

Tomorrow will be ....
On .... we usually ....
....

FIGURE 50 *Worksheet 19* – Today, Yesterday and Tomorrow

Time	Name	Doctor	Name	Doctor
8.30	Sam Ellis	Dr Watt	Chance Brow	Dr Singh
8.45	Tim Taylor	Dr Watt	Tom Brillo	Dr Singh
9.00	Rhian Attz	Dr Watt	Billy Bayer	Dr Singh
9.15	Alf Blinko	Dr Watt	Sabeen Shah	Dr Singh
9.30	Abdul Day	Dr Watt		
9.45	Sally Smith	Dr Watt	Tara Mayhew	Dr Singh
10.00	Sue Jones	Dr Watt	Simon Says	Dr Singh

Doctor's Surgery
Appointment Card

Name _____

Time _____

Doctor _____

Don't be late!

Appointment Card

Name _____

Time _____

Doctor _____

Don't be late!

FIGURE 51 *Worksheet 20* – Appointments

CHAPTER **AREA**

This chapter includes:

- Introduction
- Covering boxes
- Body prints
- Body measures
- Cotton wool balls
- Vegetables
- Shadows
- Boxes
- Letter shapes
- Grids
- Make a square metre
- Area activities for the rest of the class

The problems related to this section are:

- Make a giant ant, spider or bird to scale   (page 184)
- Make a model of the school   (page 184)
- Make a map of your classroom   (page 185)
- Make a box to carry 1 kilogram   (page 189)
- Parcels   (page 190)
- How many vital statistics can you find out about your body?   (page 191)
- Invent a new way of measuring   (page 194)
- How much space does your skin take up?   (page 199)
- How much wallpaper would you need to decorate the school?   (page 200)
- Ten metres of string   (page 200)
- Polyominoes   (page 201)

INTRODUCTION

There are a number of 'hidden' understandings that children may need to be helped with as they learn to measure in two dimensions, which can be easily overlooked. They need to understand that:

- all objects have surfaces, whether they be flat or curved;
- rectangular solids and most prisms, e.g. cubes and boxes, have flat surfaces. Whilst the children may not be able to name the shapes, they may be able to name and count the surfaces or faces;
- surface areas can be covered with anything;
- surface areas have perimeters which contain a space;
- areas can be compared and ordered.

The National Curriculum suggests certain goals at each Key Stage in the understanding of the measurement.

	Pupils should be taught to:
Key Stage 1	
Key Stage 2	**a** choose and use appropriate measuring instruments; interpret numbers and read scales to an increasing degree of accuracy
	b find areas and volumes by counting methods, leading to the use of other practical methods, *e.g. dissection*

FIGURE 52 *Key Stage goals – Area*

ACTIVITY <u>1</u> COVERING BOXES

——— LEARNING OBJECTIVES ———

1   Comparing objects using appropriate language by direct comparison.
2   Using common, non-standard units of area.
3   Finding areas by counting methods.
4   Understanding the language of comparatives.

What you will need

The children will need some old, empty cardboard boxes (it doesn't matter what size) and some pretty wrapping paper, or leftover coloured paper. They will also need access to scissors and glue.

What to do

Ask the children to cut the paper to cover each face 'exactly' and separately. This is not the same as wrapping, which allows some overlapping and allows more than one face at a time to be covered. The children may well choose to use different colours and different papers for each face.

Teachers may feel that it is appropriate to use the finished products as buildings in a display, or for junk modelling.

The children will need encouragement to find a way to make the shapes they cut out the right size. Some choose to:

- cut round the box while it is actually on the paper;
- guess and adjust;
- draw round the faces they are trying to cover:
- draw round them all, cut them out and then try to match them to where they belong.

The children will need to discuss their own and each other's methods to make decisions about the most straightforward method to use. Once they have had a chance to think about this, they can be invited to have a second try (either during the first session or on another occasion), and then decide whether or not they have improved, and *how* since their first attempt. These discussions are also a nice opportunity to develop or revisit children's awareness of the names of the shapes of each of the faces.

Organisation

If there are enough boxes, scissors and glue available, this activity can be worked with the whole class. It seems to work best with two groups, so that there is not too much paper and glue flying around. The teacher needs to be available to begin the activity, perhaps staying with the children while they fix their first face, or until they have decided on their method. Then he or she needs to be available to discuss their methods as they near completion.

The rest of the class can be usefully engaged in *Letter shapes* which requires the teacher to 'pass by' occasionally.

Activities that some children might need to do first

1   Play a game. You need a collection of boxes and a paper shape already cut to match each face of the box. Each child playing the game needs to choose a box. They then take it in turns to choose a shape that they think matches one of the faces on their box. If they are correct, they can stick the paper shape on their box. The first player to cover every face on their box wins the game. The teacher can make this game easy or difficult by selecting boxes which are very different or very similar. (SSM4a)

2   The game in activity 1 can be used as an activity rather than have the competitive element, where children simply have to choose shapes to match the faces of their box. (SSM4a)

3   *Body prints.*

Reinforcing activities that some children might need

1   Cut coloured paper into strips, oblongs and/or squares. Let the children use them to cover the faces of boxes, leaving no gaps. (SSM4a)

2   Use strips and rectangles as in activity 1, but use them to cover old postcards, Christmas cards or envelopes. (SSM4a)

3   *Letter shapes.*

Activities that some children might be ready to move on to

1   Ask the children to stick squared paper onto each face of boxes (either 1 cm² or 2 cm² paper). How many sheets of squared paper do they think they will need to cover all the surfaces?
They can go on to find out the surface area of each face (either by counting or by multiplication). Some may be able to go on to find out the total number of squares which cover their box and to order the boxes by their surface area. (SSM4a)

2   Children enjoy making guesses and finding out the surface areas of big boxes (5 cm² paper is good for a start). (SSM4a)

3   Find a big stone or log. Let the children use squared paper – this is best cut into individual squares – to find out its surface area. Can they find one or two different boxes with the same surface area? (SSM4a)

Similar activities for other measures

LENGTH
*   Use strips of card or ribbon. Let the children select or cut pieces to make a frame around old Christmas cards, postcards, pictures from magazines that they particularly like or their own pictures. Extend this to 'framing' irregularly cut pictures and outlines. (SSM4a)

CAPACITY/VOLUME
*   The children will need one large box and loads of small ones. Can they fill the large box exactly, by selecting the appropriate small ones? Extend this to children filling boxes with a single-sized box – used milk cartons are good as fillers. (SSM4a,c)

ANGLE
*   Let the children use commercially produced material, such as Pattern Blocks, to 'fill' 360° (see figure 53). Alternatively, teachers may choose to make their own set of colourful corners. Ask the children to stick them around the inside of a circle (see figure 54). (SSM3c)

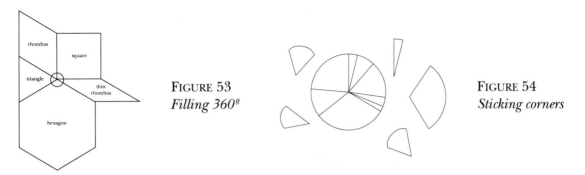

FIGURE 53
Filling 360°

FIGURE 54
Sticking corners

WEIGHT

- You will need one heavy object and lots of lighter ones – old keys, screws and other bits and bobs are good for this.

    The children need access to a balance. The heavy object is placed in one side of the balance. Ask the children to choose the appropriate smaller objects and place them in the pan until it balances exactly with the heavier object. (SSM4a)

ACTIVITY 2   BODY PRINTS

┌─────────────────── LEARNING OBJECTIVES ───────────────────┐

1   Comparing objects using appropriate language by direct comparison.
2   Using common, non-standard units of area.
3   Finding areas by counting methods.
4   Selecting and using the appropriate mathematics and materials.

└──┘

What you will need

The children may need to use a sand tray, paint, plasticine, paper and pens. They will also need cubes, money or shapes as units of measure.

What to do

Let the children develop their own book of prints. Teachers may feel that it is appropriate to use the headings shown in figure 55 to make a booklet for the children to use. They can print with paint, or draw round the outline of the part of their body they are concentrating on, or make an impression in plasticine or sand.

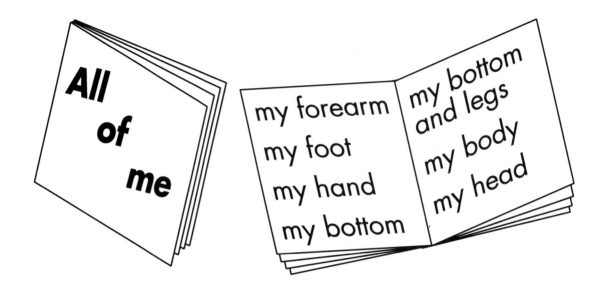

FIGURE 55 *Bodyprint booklet*

When they have their outline(s), the following questions can be posed or problems set:

- Will more cubes fit on your hand print or your footprint?
- Find the area of each part of your body (in cubes, hexagons or any other unit that seems appropriate). The children may choose different units for each part of their body. This is a good opportunity to discuss the appropriateness of different units; for example, a centimetre square is less appropriate for measuring a bottom print than it is for a hand print.

Organisation

This can be organised as a class session, with different groups of children working on the areas of different parts of their bodies.

Alternatively, this activity can be introduced to the class as a whole, with every child finding, for example, the area of their own hand print. Then the rest of the measures can be saved and used for the children to 'get on with' when the teacher wishes to work more closely with a group.

This can also be used as a group activity, where a group of children work together to produce the area statistics of one child in the group. (It is interesting enough to see how the children go about deciding who is the chosen one!) In this case, it works well as a group or a class activity. Either way, the children need to be involved in some discussion which helps them to think about how they will work together.

Activities that some children might need to do first

1   Find areas of both regular and irregular shapes using non-standard units. (SSM4a)

2   Find the area of just one part of their body. (SSM4a)

3   Choose a shape from a selection, cover it with bits, e.g. paperclips, leaves, corks. (SSM4a)

Reinforcing activities that some children might need

1   A similar activity, with the teacher as the 'thing to be measured'. (SSM4a)

2   A similar activity with a doll or teddy. (SSM4a)

3   *Covering boxes.*

Activities that some children might be ready to move on to

1   Ask them to fill one or all of their prints with pennies. How much is each bit of them worth? Who has the most expensive/cheapest foot? (SSM4a)

2   Extend this to using other coins or notes. How can they find out how much their outline is worth in £5 notes if the poor teacher only has one to lend them? (SSM4a)

3   *Body measures.*

4   *Cotton wool balls.*

Similar activities for other measures

LENGTH
•   The same worksheets can be used to make a book where the children measure the length of each of the units listed.
  – Which is the longest?
  – How many hands match the length of a body?
  – How many pennies fit along your arm? (SSM4a)
•   *Beads*
•   *Ten*

CAPACITY/VOLUME
•   The same worksheets can be used to make a book where the children measure the capacities (by displacement?) of each of the units listed. (Teachers may feel that the children would be best to try to find the capacity of their body by displacement in the bath at home and then report back. This does, however, get them involved in some complicated arithmetic.)
  – Which part of you takes up the most space?
  – Can you put your bits in order?
  – How many hands match your forearm?
  – How many pennies would fill your hand? (This can be solved by finding out how many pennies displace the same amount of water as a hand.)

Alternatively, they can use a doll as a model. (SSM4a)
- *Paint*
- *Fill a pot*
- *Sinkers*

Mass
- *Envelopes*
- *Filling boxes*

ACTIVITY 3   BODY MEASURES

┌─────────────────── LEARNING OBJECTIVES ───────────────────┐

1   Comparing objects using appropriate language by direct
     comparison.
2   Using common, non-standard units of area.
3   Finding areas by counting methods.
4   Selecting and using the appropriate mathematics and
     materials.

└───┘

What you will need

The children will need something to record their work on.

What to do

In this activity, the children will be using a variety of body parts as
units of measure. There must be an agreement with the children
about what is to be measured. This can be as straightforward as a
sheet of A1 paper, a door or a table top. Alternatively, it may be
related to a topic, e.g. an outline of a whale, or a shield, or a new
piece of carpet in the room.

The children will then need to decide which units they could
use. They will come up with a wide range of suggestions, from
hands to bottoms, and from knees to torsos. Let them decide how
many they will need for their measuring. For example, how many
children can stand in one car parking space? How many can kneel,
sit, lie down, crouch, etc., in the same space? How many hands will
fit in the same space?

The outcomes of this can lead to some useful discussion about
the need for standard units of measure.

Organisation

The larger the space, the more children you will need for the measuring, unless the children themselves come up with an alternative method. They tend to be excited by measuring large spaces, so if this is used as a starting point, the children are often enthused to go on and measure slightly smaller spaces themselves.

We recommend introducing the idea to the whole class, and allowing them to be part of the first 'big' measure. If there are some capable organisers available in the group, they can be appointed to direct the rest of the children. If not, the teacher will need to take suggestions from the children and act upon them.

Other challenges, which teachers may choose to give to pairs or groups of children (four seems to be plenty, even in a class of angels!), have been included in the worksheet on page 178, and can be cut up into individual challenge cards.

Activities that some children might need to do first

1   Find areas of smaller, regular shapes using non-standard units. (SSM4a)

2   *Boxes.*

3   *Body prints.*

Reinforcing activities that some children might need

1   See activity in the reinforcement section of *Boxes* on page 167.

2   Let the children decide on and use personal body prints or outlines to measure with. Let them have a chat about how many they think they will use in advance of actually measuring, and how they are making their estimates, e.g. are they imagining how many will fit in half the space and then doubling that number? They will appreciate an opportunity to change their estimate along the way. They may choose to use:
    • handspans (these can be printed, or drawn round, or cut out and stuck);
    • footprints (these can be printed, or drawn round, or cut out and stuck);
    • finger prints (these can be printed, or children may feel that it's useful to cover a smaller area with finger prints (e.g. a playing card) and then use that as the unit of measure. (SSM4a)

3   *Cotton wool balls.*

Activities that some children might be ready to move on to

1   Ask the children to estimate and check how many newspapers, or sheets of newspaper, they will need to: cover the floor, wall, hall, playground, corridor. (SSM4a)

2   Ask the children to estimate, and then justify their estimates, how many elephants, cars, buses will fit in the classroom, in the hall, in the car park, etc. (SSM4a)

3   *Letter shapes.*

4   *Vegetables.*

Similar activities for other measures

LENGTH
- This activity can be adapted so that children are using body parts as units of linear measure. The following challenges can be set:
  - Use handspans to measure the length and width of your table.
  - Use footprints to measure the length and width of your book corner.
  - How many children could lie down across your classroom floor?
  - How many children could sit in a line across the width of the hall? With their legs crossed? With their legs stretched?
  - How many children can kneel round the edge of a sheet of A1 paper?
  - How many children can sit along your desk? (SSM4a)
- *Beads*
- *Ten*

CAPACITY/VOLUME
- *Paint*
- *Fill a pot*
- *Sinkers*

MASS
- *Envelopes*
- *Filling boxes*

ACTIVITY 4   COTTON WOOL BALLS

LEARNING OBJECTIVES
---

1   Comparing objects using appropriate language by direct comparison.
2   Using common, non-standard units of area.
3   Finding areas by counting methods.
4   Using a variety of forms of mathematical representation.

What you will need

The children will need loads of cotton wool balls and some interesting shapes to paint.

What to do

Ask the children to use one cotton wool ball to spread paint. Of a collection of different shapes and spaces, estimate which you could cover with one ballful. Let the children work on a large Carroll diagram and sort the shapes according to the rules shown in figure 56.

	I think these shapes will need more than two ballfuls of paint to cover them.	I think these shapes will not need more than two ballfuls of paint to cover them.
These shapes actually need more than two ballfuls of paint to cover them.		
These shapes do not actually need more than two ballfuls of paint to cover them.		

FIGURE 56 *A Carroll diagram of ballfuls.*

Offer a collection of shapes for them to use, and let them sort them according to the criteria on the top line only.

When they have made their guesses, let the children paint their shapes and move them into the appropriate part of the diagram according to the labels at the side. They will need to find a way to keep a record of the number of ballfuls they have used – they can write the number on the back of the shapes.

Discuss the outcomes with them:

- Which ones did you guess correctly?
- What can you say about the shapes in the bottom right-hand space?
- Which shapes need more than two ballfuls of paint to cover them?
  (This activity works just as well if a paintbrushful of paint is used as a unit of measure.)

Organisation

This activity works best as a group activity, with children working individually or in pairs, although the teacher does not need to work with them all the time. The teacher needs to be available to introduce the activity, and to discuss their estimates with them. They then need the opportunity to discuss the outcomes of their painting and to compare them with the results of others.

It is a useful learning opportunity if children not only interpret their own diagrams, but also those of their peers.

The rest of the class might be engaged in one of the activities at the end of the section (see page 176).

Activities that some children might need to do first

1   Unroll one cotton wool ball. What is the largest area you can make it cover with no gaps? Set a collection of tasks, for example:
   • How many rolled-up balls will you need to cover a paper plate?
   • How many unrolled balls? (SSM4a)

2   Use cotton wool balls for printing. (SSM4a)

3   Let the children make their own wrapping paper by using a sheet of paper and sponges to print a design with. Extend to setting particular criteria, for example:
   • Choose a sponge which covers your paper in twelve splodges.
   • Choose two sponges which can make a design which covers your paper with no gaps. (SSM4a)

4   *Vegetables.*

Reinforcing activities that some children might need

1   Let the children estimate how many cotton wool balls they will need to cover a leaf, a hand print or a footprint or a paper ice-cream cone. Talk about their estimates:
   • Who needed more balls? How many more?
   • Who needed to put balls back? How many?
   • Who took loads too many?
   • Who was nearly right?
   • How many did you use?
   • Who needed the most/least number of balls? (SSM4a)

2   *Paint.*

Activities that some children might be ready to move on to

1   *Letter shapes.*

2   *Boxes.*

3   *Shadows.*

Similar activities for other measures

Mass
   • *Envelopes*

ACTIVITY <u>5</u>   VEGETABLES

```
┌──────────────── LEARNING OBJECTIVES ────────────────┐
│                                                       │
│  1  'Comparing objects using appropriate language by direct │
│       comparison.                                     │
│  2   Using common, non-standard units of area and estimating │
│       with those units.                               │
│  3   Finding areas by counting methods.               │
│  4   Understanding the language of comparatives.       │
│                                                       │
└───────────────────────────────────────────────────────┘
```

What you will need

The children will need a selection of green leafy vegetables, such as Brussels sprouts, cabbage, lettuce, and some scrap paper or newspaper and scissors.

What to do

Ask the children to:

- select a vegetable;
- cut a piece of paper that they think will be the right size to stick all the leaves of the vegetable on individually;
- try it to see how close they were.

It is a good idea for the teacher to try this too! The outcome is always very surprising, and it makes the children feel better if the teacher's guess was appalling too!

Discuss the results with the children:

- Do all the sprouts cover the same area?
- How many sprouts would you need to fill the same space as a cabbage?
- How many lettuces would you need to make lettuce wallpaper to cover our walls?
- How many cabbages would you need to make a cabbage table cloth?

(It is a good idea to find some rabbits, pigs or horses that the used vegetables can be sent to, so that they aren't wasted.)

Organisation

Because this is quite an unusual activity, the children are particularly interested in it. The element of 'competition' with the teacher works well too. So we recommend that this is a class activity, with the children working in pairs. The only disadvantage to that is if the classroom is very restricted for desk space, because a decent-sized cabbage takes about one sheet of a tabloid newspaper.

Activities that some children might need to do first

1   *Boxes.*

2   *Body prints.*

Reinforcing activities that some children might need

1   *Boxes* reinforcements.

2   *Cotton wool balls* and reinforcements.

Activities that some children might be ready to move on to

1   *Boxes* extensions.

2   *Cotton wool balls* extensions.

3   *Body measures.*

4   If the children can use knives, they can try challenges such as:
    • Cut a potato so it covers the largest area possible.
    • Try other vegetables.
    • Which covers the most space, a potato or a parsnip? (SSM4a)

Similar activities for other measures

LENGTH
• Use vegetables as a unit of linear measure. Ask questions and set challenges like:
    – How far will ten carrots reach?
    – What is the longest line you can make with the leaves of one Brussels sprout?
    – Measure yourself with carrots. Use carrots or make a stick model of one person in your group. (SSM4a)

CAPACITY/VOLUME
• Use a selection of vegetables and ask the children to order them by the amount of space they take up. They will need to be able to appreciate measurement by displacement, and to have the opportunity to discuss the best method of measuring and recording. (SSM4a)
• Use vegetables as fillers for a string bag or a shoe box. How many potatoes will fit in the bag? How many carrots? cabbages? (SSM4a)

MASS
• *Envelopes*

ACTIVITY <u>6</u>   SHADOWS

What you will need

One very large sheet of paper, or several A1 sheets, some thick felt
pens and a sunny day.

What to do ·

Ask the children to work in pairs. Let them decide on one of the
pair to be the 'measurer' and the other to be the 'measuree'. They
will need one large sheet of paper between them.

The child whose shadow is to be measured will need to stand in
the centre of the paper. The other child should draw round the feet
on the paper to ensure that, throughout the activity, the measuree
always stands on exactly the same spot.

The children will need to mark the outline of their paper on the
ground with chalk or bricks to ensure that the paper is always laid
down on the same spot.

Every hour, on the hour, during the school day, the pairs of
children will need to go outside, arrange their paper, and the
'measuree' into the correct position and draw round their shadow.

Ask them to choose a suitable unit (they may suggest
handprints, circles, playing cards, etc.) and find the areas of the
shadows after each measure. Teachers may feel that it is appropriate
to record these results as numbers or graphically, e.g. a line graph.

The next day, these results can be viewed and discussed:

- When did the shadow have the largest/smallest area?
- Did any two shadows have similar areas?
- What do you think the next shadow would be like?
- Why do you think it changes?
- What do you think will happen tomorrow?

Organisation

The decision on organisation for this activity must rest with the teacher and depend on the way the class works, but we suggest the following alternatives:

- The whole class working in pairs and going outside together every hour. Teachers have to steel themselves to the fact that this activity alone will dominate the day, with only time left for bits and pieces of work such as *Letter shapes* or *Boxes* in between.
- Again, have the whole class working on the same activity, arrange them into groups of five or six, but ask only two children from the group to be involved in going outside and recording the shadows. The rest of the group can be involved in finding the areas of the shadows and presenting the findings graphically. This is a rather good way to organise the activity if teachers are trying to encourage groups of children to co-operate as a team.
- Organise the children as above but just have one group working on the activity, while the rest of the class are involved in a more static task, such as *Letter shapes*, *Vegetables* or *Grids*.
- Organise just two children to measure the shadows, but expect them to report back to the rest of the class on their findings.

Activities that some children might need to do first

1 *Boxes.*

2 *Body measures.*

3 Let the children find the area of a sheet of newspaper in boxes, yoghurt pots, or anything else they choose. Make it more complicated by using different-sized papers. Use the junk to print with, then count the prints. Discuss with them the most appropriate unit for their measurements, and the need for standard measure. Extend this idea to using a roll of wallpaper – do they need to print on the whole roll to find the area? (SSM4a)

Reinforcing activities that some children might need

1 *Vegetables.*

2 *Body prints.*

Activities that some children might be ready to move on to

1 *Make a square metre.*

2 Use a square metre of paper or card to make a giant tangram. Let the children experiment with the pieces to make some giant pictures. (SSM4a)

3 *Covering boxes.*

Similar activities for other measures

LENGTH

- Instead of using a child as the shadow-maker, use a stick and measure the length of it at hourly intervals. The children will need to ensure that the stick and the paper are in the same place each time, as described in the Area activity. There are two advantages of approaching this activity as a linear one. The first is that if the 'lengths' are subsequently transferred onto a line graph, the children then have an immediate comparison of what they saw. (Teachers may prefer to ask the children to cut lengths of ribbon or paper strips to the same length as the shadow and then transfer these directly on to a graph.)

    The second advantage is that, if the lines are drawn at hourly (or even half hourly) intervals throughout the school day, the outcome can then be used as a clock for the next few days. After that, it will lose its accuracy, the reasons for which may be a useful discussion point. (SSM4a)

CAPACITY/VOLUME

- *Paint*
- *Fill a pot*
- *Sinkers*

MASS

- *Envelopes*
- *Plasticine models*

ACTIVITY 7   BOXES

┌─────────────── LEARNING OBJECTIVES ───────────────┐

1   Comparing objects using appropriate language by direct comparison.
2   Using common, non-standard units of area.
3   Choosing units appropriate to a situation.
4   Finding areas by counting methods.
5   Using a variety of forms of mathematical presentation.

└──┘

What you will need

The children will need some boxes containing a wide variety of objects:

FIGURE 57 *Covering shapes*

- a sorting box with a collection of flat items that the children can find the area of, such as box lids, magazines, workbooks, reading books, old postcards, squares, circles, triangles and some irregular shapes;
- a covering box containing a variety of items they can use to cover with: bricks, cubes, paper clips, counters, conkers, shells, old postcards, etc.;
- some large sheets of paper for drawing Carroll diagrams and tree diagrams.

What to do

OPTION 1

Let the children choose five things from the sorting box. Let them also choose something to cover them with, e.g. shells. Ask them to:

- write on a post-it note how many paper clips they think they will need to cover each surface and stick the post-it note on top of the appropriate shape (see figure 57);
- cover them to see how close they were;
- either put them in order according to how good their guesses were, or p\ut them in order according to how many paperclips covered each object.

OPTION 2

Let the children sort some of the items in the sorting box. They can record their work by placing them on a large Carroll or tree diagram. (For further information on Carroll and tree diagrams, please refer to the glossary.) The children may be able to choose their own rules, or they might need to use one of the following:

- Needs more than fifteen bricks to cover it./Does not need more than fifteen bricks to cover it.
- Has a greater area than a postcard./Does not have a greater area than a postcard.
- I need more than ten to cover my desk./I would not need more than ten to cover my desk.

OPTION 3

Let the children find ten items in the sorting box which can be covered with between twenty and thirty units (any units from the covering box will do as long as they need between twenty and thirty of them).

Organisation

If there are plenty of sorting boxes and plenty of 'coverers', this task works well as a class activity, with the children working either individually or in pairs. Teachers will need to give the children the opportunity to help each other, in thinking about their estimates, and in studying each others' sorting. If they do this, it takes some of the demand off the teacher's time. Then the teacher needs to be available to pass by and encourage the children to invent challenging sorts.

Alternatively, teachers may prefer to let a group of six to eight children work individually or in pairs on this activity while the rest of the class either tries one of the activities at the end of the section in pairs or is engaged in another reasonably independent task.

Activities that some children might need to do first

1   Estimate first and accurately cover any flat surface, e.g. floor, footprint, book, with newspaper or cubes. (SSM4a)

2   Discover whether the way you organise 'coverers' makes a difference to the count, i.e. do higgledy piggledy arrangements give you a different number than if you arrange things in an orderly fashion? (SSM4a)

3   *Body prints.*

Reinforcing activities that some children might need

1   A game for two players. Let each child take it in turns to:
   • Take an item from the sorting box and choose a unit to cover it with, e.g. bricks.
   • The same person decides whether their partner needs to find another surface which needs more/fewer or the same number of bricks to cover it.
   • The second player follows instructions.
   • Both players cover their surface.
   • If the second player was right, they keep their item from the sorting box.
   • The player with the most items from the box after eight rounds wins the game.
      This game can be changed so that players take it in turns to take two things from the sorting box. Their partner must find something which needs to be covered with fewer than the largest of these, and more than the smallest of these, i.e. one which is between them in area. (SSM4a)

2   Play 'Guess and count'. Let the children take it in turns to:
   • take something from the sorting box;
   • choose a unit from the covering box;
   • guess how many units they will need to cover their surface.
If they are right, they keep the item from the sorting box. The winner is the player with the most items from the sorting box after eight rounds. (SSM4a)

Activities that some children might be ready to move on to

1 Play 'Cover it'. Players choose something from the sorting box as their game board. They take it in turns to choose one object from the covering box. (They do not need to choose the same thing each time!) The winner is the first player to cover their surface completely. (SSM4a)

2 Play 'Two the same'. Players take it in turns to:
   * choose two items from the sorting box which they think will have the same area;
   * test to see if they were right by placing one on top of the other, or by finding the areas by choosing and using a unit of measure.

   If they were right, they keep them; if not, they put them back. The player with the most things from the sorting box at the end of five rounds wins the game. (SSM4a)

3 *Covering boxes.*

Similar activities for other measures

LENGTH
* *Beads*
* *Ten*
* *Sorting box*
* *How long?*
* *Plasticine sausages*
* *Bodies*
* *Detectives*
* *Make a line*

CAPACITY/VOLUME
* *Paint*
* *Fill a pot*
* *Sinkers*

WEIGHT
* *Envelopes*
* *Plasticine models*

ACTIVITY 8 LETTER SHAPES

┌───┐
LEARNING OBJECTIVES

1 Comparing objects using appropriate language by direct comparison.
2 Using common standard units of area.
3 Choosing units appropriate to a situation.
4 Finding areas by counting methods.
5 Discussing work, responding to and asking mathematical questions.
└───┘

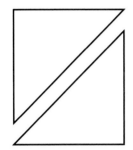

FIGURE 58   *Squares*

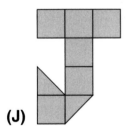

(J)

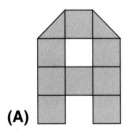

(A)

FIGURE 59   *Shapes*

What you will need

The children will need a lot of 3 centimetre x 3 centimetre squares and halves made by cutting the 3 centimetre squares in half diagonally (see figure 58).

What to do

This is an activity for each of the children to try on their own. Let the children experiment with the shapes by asking them questions like:

- Can you make a snake?
- Can you make a square?
- Can you make a zig-zag line?

Then set them the challenge of making their first initial using the shapes. They usually decide on shapes like the ones shown in figure 59.
    Can they work out the number of square units they have used for this letter by putting the halves together to make whole ones where possible and appropriate?
    Discuss with the group what they have done:

- How many different letters have been made?
- If two people made the same letter, did they make them the same way? Did they have the same area?
- Which letter has the largest/smallest area?
- Are there any two letters which have the same area?

Organisation

The children work best at this activity if they do the first task on their own. They will need to have cut themselves plenty of squares and halves in advance, otherwise the lack of shapes changes what they do. After they have got to grips with the idea of making letters with the shapes (some may need a few examples to start them off!), they can either continue to work individually to make their names or to work with a partner to make both the names.

Activities that some children might need to do first

1   Make letters with interlocking cubes or Polydron. (SSM4a)

2   Make shapes with whole squares, i.e. join the shapes to make a square, rectangle, turrets, frames, etc. (SSM4a)

3   *Cotton wool balls.*

Reinforcing activities that some children might need

1   Let the children make their whole name and find the total area. Ask similar questions to those in **What to do** above:
    • Are there any two names which have the same area?
    • Which name has the largest/smallest area?
    Sort the names. These can be recorded on Carroll, Venn or tree diagrams. The children may like to make up their own rules or use one of these:
    • Has an area greater than fifty units./Does not have an area greater than fifty units.
    • Uses more than five halves./Does not use more than five halves. (SSM4a)

2   Collect information about the children's names and use a database to sort and find information about them. (SSM4a)

3   *Boxes.*

Activities that some children might be ready to move on to

1   Let the class or a group make all the letters of the alphabet and find the area of each, and the total. Ask similar questions to those above:
    • Which letter has the largest/smallest area?
    • Are there any two letters which have the same area?
    Sort the letters. This work can be recorded as above with similar rules. (SSM4a,c)

2   Use the sheet on page 179 and cut it into individual cards.
    The children will need a die or spinner with the following faces or spaces: 0, $\frac{1}{2}$, 1, 1 $\frac{1}{2}$, 2, 2 $\frac{1}{2}$. They take it in turns to:
    • roll the die or spin the spinner;
    • take the appropriate number of shapes and place them on their picture.
    The player with the first complete picture wins the game. The children will need to make up their own rules about whether they can have any spare shapes or not.
       Alternatively, the children can stick down the shapes they used to make their name, and use this as a game board. Playing this game often generates some useful discussion about whether or not it is fair. If they think that it is an unfair game, teachers may wish to encourage them to change it to make it fair. (SSM4a,c)

Similar activities for other measures

LENGTH
• *Beads*
• *Ten*
• *Sorting box*
• *How long?*
• *Plasticine sausages*
• *Bodies*
• *Detectives*
• *Make a line*

CAPACITY/VOLUME
• *Paint*
• *Fill a pot*
• *Sinkers*

WEIGHT
• *Envelopes*
• *Plasticine models*

ACTIVITY 9   # GRIDS

┌─────────────── LEARNING OBJECTIVES ───────────────┐

1   Choosing appropriate standard units of area and making
     sensible estimates with them in everyday situations.
2   Extending understanding of the relationship between units.
3   Finding areas by counting methods.
4   Developing mathematical strategies and looking for ways
     to overcome difficulties.

└──┘

What you will need

The teacher or the children will need to make three sets of all the
different shapes possible from one, two, three and four squares
(paper is fine, but card is better in case someone sneezes!). These
can be made from centimetre squared paper, 2 centimetre squared
paper, 5 centimetre squared paper, decimetres or interlocking
cubes. (Worksheets are offered on pages 180 and 181.) The
children will also need a spinner with the numbers one to four,
and a five-by-five grid for each player.

What to do

Teach the children to play a grid game. Each player needs a board,
and there should be plenty of the shapes they have made available.
Players should:

* take it in turns to spin the spinner;
* take a shape with the appropriate number of squares;
* place their shape on their board.

The first player to fill their grid with shapes is the winner. The
players must decide whether or not they are going to allow each
other to move the pieces around on the board during play. It
doesn't matter what they decide, as long as they all stick to the rules!

Organisation

Teachers may choose to use either of the following ways of
introducing this game to the class.

OPTION 1

As a class activity, where children work in groups of between two and four to make their game. Then, as each group is ready, the teacher can explain the game to them. This has the advantage of having groups of children who have finished making the game and have played it a couple of times, who are then available to explain the rules to others as they become ready. If the whole class is playing together, the teacher may choose to stop them occasionally to swap groups around, so winners can play winners, and 'runners up' can play 'runners up'.

OPTION 2

As a group activity, while the other children are involved in similar activities, such as *Letter shapes*. One group of children can make a 'best' version of the game, which is decorated and laminated, then they can either write out the rules for others to use, or one of the 'chosen few' can explain the game to other groups.

Activities that some children might need to do first

1   A simpler version of the game can be made, using shapes made from only one, two or three squares. (SSM4a)

2   *Make a square metre.*

Reinforcing activities that some children might need

1   *Letter shapes* and extensions.

2   Play on a larger grid – the children will need more pieces. (SSM4a,c)

3   Ask the children to change the rules as they see fit. This can develop into an interesting writing exercise, if the children are subsequently expected to write an account of their rules! (SSM4a,c)

Activities that some children might be ready to move on to

1   Extend the game to using different gameboards rather than using a square grid. (SSM4a,c)

2   Change the game so that each child needs to make a shape with a specific area, for example, 36 square centimetres. (SSM4a,c)

3   Extend the game further by allowing half squares (a half square being made by cutting diagonally across a square). (SSM4a,c)

Similar activities for other measures

WEIGHT
- *Filling boxes*
- *Kilogram collections*

ACTIVITY 10 MAKE A SQUARE METRE

┌─────────────── LEARNING OBJECTIVES ───────────────┐

1   Choosing appropriate standard units of area and making
     sensible estimates with them in everyday situations.
2   Extending understanding of the relationship between units.
3   Finding areas by counting methods.
4   Selecting and using appropriate mathematics and materials.

└──┘

What you will need

The children will need plenty of square decimetres, made from thin
card, and a metre stick.

What to do

Let the children decorate the decimetres with anything they choose:
sticky paper, magazine pictures, paint, crayon. Use Blu-tak or drawing
pins to join enough of them together to make a square metre.
    Invite the children to comment on the square they have made.

- How many rows are there?
- How many in each row?
- How many from corner to corner?
- How many decimetres did they need?
- Is there a quick way to find out? (Ten rows of ten makes 100.)
- How far do they think they would reach if we placed them all
  end to end? one above the other? two by two? three by three?

Organisation

This works best as a class lesson. Let all the children decorate as
many or as few square decimetres as speedily or as slowly as they
like, and then add them to the square as they are complete. Any

spares can be used as bookmarks! It may be appropriate to appoint a couple of children as 'square-makers' who can be responsible for actually making the square.

When the square is complete, all the children can sit by it, admire it and join in the discussion.

Activities that some children might need to do first

1   The Area ideas which follow *Make a line.* (SSM4a,c; UA2c)

2   *Grids.*

3   *Letter shapes.*

Reinforcing activities that some children might need

1   Take all the squares down. In pairs, let other children re-assemble it on different occasions and in different places, e.g. on the floor, on the desk, on the wall, in the corridor. (SSM4a,c)

2   Let the children play *Make a square metre.* Two to four children can play. They should take it in turns to roll a die. Collect the appropriate number of squares and use them towards building the metre square. The player who completes the square wins the game.

Alternatively, players can build their own metre square, but you need loads of decimetres for this, and it works better if they use a spinner with numbers zero to nine. (SSM4a,c)

Activities that some children might be ready to move on to

1   Draw round one of the decimetres on centimetre squared paper. How many squares does it cover? Number them. Can the children work out how many centimetre squares would be needed to make the metre square? (Let them find their own methods.) (SSM4a,c)

2   Extend the *Make a metre* game, so that children need to collect centimetre squares (or Centicubes) and trade them for a decimetre square. They will need to invent some new rules to hurry the game along, e.g. using two or three dice, or using a special spinner, or using a set of number cards. (SSM4a,c)

Similar activities for other measures

LENGTH
- Use 10 centimetre strips of card and set similar challenges:
    1   Decorate them and join them into lengths of 1 metre. (SSM4a,c)

2 Discuss the metres that have been made:
  – How many strips were needed for each metre?
  – How many completed ones did we make?
  – How many could we have made if we had coloured two strips each? Three?
  – Can you find/see anything longer than, shorter than, the same length as the metre we have made? (SSM4a,b)

3 Let some children (pairs is probably enough) fasten the metres together. (They will need to take care not to overlap them!) (SSM4a)

4 They can still play *Make a metre* and extend it to using centimetres. (SSM4a,b)
- *Metre mouse*
- *How high?*

CAPACITY/VOLUME

- Ask the children to make 10 decimetre cubes from card. (This will hold exactly one litre of material, incidentally.) For obvious reasons, sand or rice are better than water as fillers. This is difficult!

  Decorate them and join them to make a cubic metre. It is probably best if several classes join forces to do this, or Multibase material blocks can be used to supplement supplies of decimetre cubes.

  They can still play *Make a (cubic) metre*, but they will probably need more than one die.
- *Blanket box*
- *Fill a litre*
- *Elastic bands*
- *200 grams of plasticine*
- *Guess which box*

MASS

- *Weigh yourself*
- *Popcorn*
- *How many stones?*
- *Gravel balance*

ANGLE

- *Flowers*

TIME

- *Digital display*

AREA ACTIVITIES FOR THE REST OF THE CLASS

These ideas are designed for children to use with little support from the teacher, other than initial clarification. Teachers may choose to turn them into worksheets or challenge cards, or simply to explain to the children what is expected of them.

1   Cut out enough footprints to cover one sheet of paper. Stick them. Count them. Did you have enough? (SSM4c)

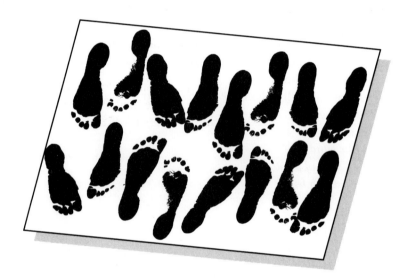

FIGURE 60 *Footprints*

2   Use sticky circles and one sheet of A4 paper. Stick the circles on. They must touch. Fit as many as you can on one sheet of paper. Use another sheet of paper. Stick the circles on. They must touch. Fit as few as you can on one sheet of paper. (SSM4c)

3   Use big cartons. Use old birthday or Christmas cards, or postcards to cover the surface completely. (A tower of these makes a good totem pole!) (SSM4c)

4   Three children need to work together to make enough square decimetres to make a square metre. (It doesn't have to be a square!) (SSM4c)

5   Cut out the shapes indicated in Figure 61. Use one, two or three of them to make:

- two parallelograms
- three hexagons
- three pentagons
- four quadrilaterals
- two different ones

The sides must touch. Draw round each shape as you make it. (SSM2bc, 4c)

6   Make as many different rectangles as you can with an area of 48 square centimetres. Record them on 2 centimetre squared paper. (SSM2bc, 4c)

7   Use a geoboard:

- How many triangles of different areas can be made?
- How many different triangles with the same area can be made?
- How many quadrilaterals of different areas can be made?

(SSM2b, 4c)

8   Use a geoboard. How many different triangles with a base of three can be made? Record their heights and their areas. Is there a rule? (SSM2b, 4c)

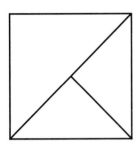

FIGURE 61 *Leading diagonal*

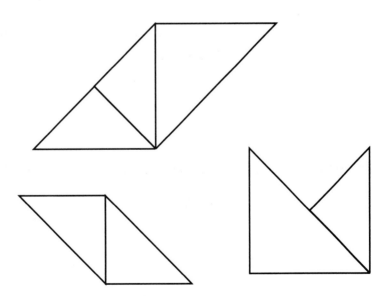

FIGURE 62 *Some answers!*

Use handspans to measure the area of your table.

Use footprints to measure the area of
your book corner.

How many children could lie down on
your classroom floor?

How many children could sit in the hall?

How many children can kneel on a
sheet of A4 paper?

How many children can sit on your desk?

Use handspans to measure the area of your chair.

FIGURE 63 *Worksheet 21 – Body measures*

Hodder & Stoughton © 1996 Janine Blinko and Ann Slater Teaching Measures. The publishers grant permission for multiple copies of this worksheet to be made in the place of purchase for use solely in that institution.

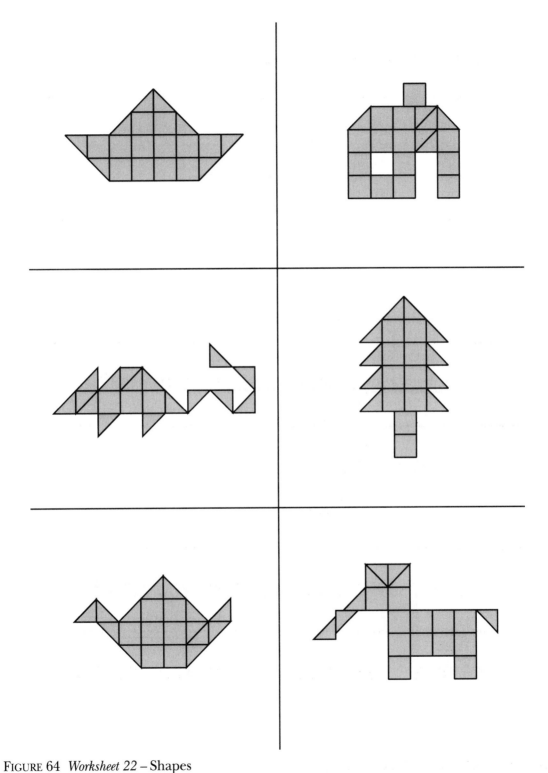

FIGURE 64 *Worksheet 22 – Shapes*
Hodder & Stoughton © 1996 Janine Blinko and Ann Slater Teaching Measures. The publishers grant permission for multiple copies of this worksheet to be made in the place of purchase for use solely in that institution.

FIGURE 65 *Worksheet 23* – Grids 1

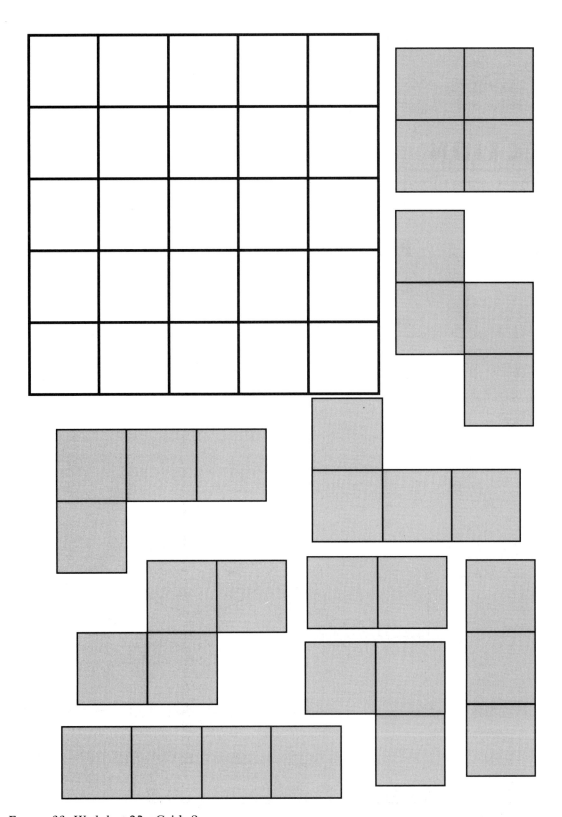

FIGURE 66 *Worksheet 23* – Grids 2

SECTION

PROBLEMS AND INVESTIGATIONS

This section is divided into two chapters:

CHAPTER 10
Organising the problems in the classroom

CHAPTER 11
Problems

CHAPTER

ORGANISING THE PROBLEMS IN THE CLASSROOM

Many of these problems can be undertaken by the whole class at the same time. The exceptions would be those which require a lot of equipment or a lot of space. The discussion with the teacher is essential, particularly as they begin the activity, when the children's interpretation of the problem may need support and possibilities for solving it will most likely need airing. The input required by the teacher very much depends on the children's previous experience of, and their confidence in working responsibly on, such open problems. In some cases, they will be able to work quite independently; in others, they may well need support every step of the way! Either way, their independence increases if they are allowed to make some mistakes and to find a way to correct them themselves, or even to see the need to start again!

These problems aim to achieve two things:

- to give children an interesting environment in which they can explore the use of the measuring skills they have/are acquiring;
- to allow children to respond to situations in different ways, and to take control of the direction they might take.

Teachers may choose to offer children a choice or two of three problems, and to expect them to find the materials they need.

All these activities address the following statements from the 'Shape, Space and Measures' section of the Key Stage 2 Programmes of Study:

Pupils should be taught to:

4a   choose appropriate standard units of length, mass, capacity and time, and make sensible estimates with them in everyday situations; extend their understanding of the relationship between units; convert one metric unit to another; know the rough metric equivalents of imperial units still in daily use;

4b   choose and use appropriate measuring instruments; interpret numbers and read scales to an increasing degree of accuracy.

CHAPTER 11   PROBLEMS

1 MAKE A GIANT ANT, SPIDER OR BIRD TO SCALE

LENGTH, AREA, SCALE
This activity gives children experience of estimating and measuring in millimetres, and choosing and using an appropriate scale.

Before they start

The children need to be reasonably competent in simple multiplication, with or without a calculator, and to have some knowledge of millimetres and their relationship to centimetres and metres. They also need to have access to some good photographs of the animals or insects they are going to make a model of or, better still, some real-life examples.

Discuss

- Which measurements do you need to know?
- What will you use to make your model?
- How will you take your measurements?
- How big will you make your model?
- How will you decide on how long the legs should be?

•	Using and Applying Mathematics	2c;3a;4b
•	Shape, Space and Measures	4a,b,c

2 MAKE A MODEL OF THE SCHOOL

LENGTH, AREA, SCALE
This activity gives children experience of estimating and measuring length and area, and making decisions about reasonable use of scale.

Before they start

The children need to be able to measure and calculate in metres and centimetres.

Discuss

- What shape is the school if you look down from above?
- Are all the buildings joined together?
- Is there an upstairs?
- How will you measure to the ceiling or the roof?
- Will you need to plan your work first?
- How much card do you think you will need?

• Using and Applying Mathematics	2a,d;3a
• Shape, Space and Measures	4a,b,c

3   MAKE A MAP OF YOUR CLASSROOM

LENGTH, AREA, SCALE, DIRECTION
This activity gives children experience of choosing and using appropriate units of measure and scale. The map can be of anything: the school, a street, a route to school.

Before they start

The children need to be very familiar with, and be able to discuss the measurement of, whatever they are planning to make a map of.

Discuss

- What measurements do you need to take?
- What do you need to know about the corners?
- What scale will you use? (e.g. a thumb length is equivalent to 10 metres, or 1 centimetre is equivalent to 100 metres.)
- Devise some questions so someone else can use your map (e.g. a treasure hunt, directing someone to their chair).

• Using and Applying Mathematics	2b,d;3b
• Shape, Space and Measures	4a,b,c

4 HOW MUCH WATER WILL FILL UP THE CLASSROOM?

CAPACITY, VOLUME, LENGTH, AREA
This activity gives children experience of calculating capacities or volumes.

Before they start

The children need to have an understanding of what a cubic metre is.

Discuss

- How many cubic metres could we stand on the floor?
- How many layers could we make?
- How can we find out how many will fill the room?
- What shall we do about the spare bits?
- How much water will fill the hall? your home?
- How much water is in the swimming pool?
- How much will all that water weigh?

• Using and Applying Mathematics	2a,c;4b,d
• Shape, Space and Measures	4a,b,c

5 MAKE A SET OF WEIGHTS

WEIGHT, VOLUME
This activity gives children experience of non-standard units of weight and volume, and the relationship between the two.

Before they start

The children need to have used a balance, and had a little experience of weighing using non-standard units.

Discuss

- What will you use to make your weights? (Plasticine, yoghurt pots with gravel in them, matchboxes with sand in them and fastened together.)
- Are you going to make every possible weight (e.g. 10 grams, 20 grams, etc.)?

- How will you make sure they are accurate?
- What will you use them for?
- Can you make up some problems for someone else to use them with?

•	Using and Applying Mathematics	3a,c;4b
•	Shape, Space and Measures	4a,b,c

6 HOW MUCH DOES YOUR HOUSE WEIGH?

LENGTH, AREA, VOLUME, WEIGHT
This problem offers children an environment to explore heavy weights.

Before they start

They all need to have had experience of handling the smallish weights in the components of a house, e.g. a brick, a bucket of concrete, a plank of wood. They need to be able to find a way to count the bricks and planks of wood. They also need to have the understanding that two approximate halves of a brick will weigh about the same as one whole one.

Discuss

- What materials is a house made of?
- Should we include the weight of the furniture?
- Should we include the weight of the people?
- Why might we want to know what a house weighs?
- What about other types of houses, blocks of flats, houses from other countries?
- Do bungalows weigh more than houses?
- Do big houses always weigh more than small ones?
- Are modern houses heavier than old ones?

•	Using and Applying Mathematics	2c,d;3a
•	Shape, Space and Measures	4a,b,c

7   HOW MUCH DO YOU DRINK IN A DAY?

CAPACITY, TIME

This activity gives children experience of estimating and measuring capacities, and of data collection and representation. The children can solve this problem at different levels, some by giving a numerical answer, others by collecting a quantity together.

Before they start

They need to have had experience of measuring capacities in litres and millilitres.

Discuss

- How many drinks do you have in a day?
- How much in each drink?
- Are they all the same amount?
- Does everyone drink the same amount?
- Does everyone have the same number of drinks?
- Do adults drink more than children?
- How will you record what you have found out?
- How much do you drink in a week? A month? A year? In your life?

• Using and Applying Mathematics		2b,d;4b
• Shape, Space and Measures		4a,b

8   DRIPPING TAP

CAPACITY, TIME

This activity gives children experience of estimating and measuring liquid capacities, and of calculating them.

Before they start

The children need to find a dripping tap and work out how much water is lost in five minutes. They need to be able to measure capacities of liquid, and to calculate them with and/or without the use of a calculator.

Discuss

- Is the dripping consistent?
- How much water will be lost in an hour? in a day? in a week?
- Suppose everyone in your street had a dripping tap for a year – how much water would be lost in the year?
- Would it be best to fix the tap? Find out how.

•	Using and Applying Mathematics	3b;4c,d
•	Shape, Space and Measures	4a,b

9   DOES THE CLASS WEIGH A TONNE?

LENGTH, AREA, CAPACITY, WEIGHT
This activity gives children experience of relating their own weight to other children's, and to other things.

Before they start

The children need to have had experience of handling smaller weights, e.g. kilograms, and of weighing themselves and each other.

Discuss

- Could we answer this question without weighing everyone?
- How can we record the information we have?
- What else might weigh the same as we do?
- What else might weigh a tonne?
- Does the class next door weigh a tonne? more than us? less than us?
- Do the teachers weigh a tonne?
- Does the whole school weigh a tonne?

•	Using and Applying Mathematics	2c,d;3a
•	Shape, Space and Measures	4a,b

10 MAKE A BOX TO CARRY 1 KILOGRAM

LENGTH, VOLUME, WEIGHT
This activity gives children experience of the relationship between different aspects of measure.

Before they start

The children need to identify what they are going to use to measure 1 kilogram. They might all choose something different, e.g. conkers, stones, polystyrene chips, water, sand, keys, paper tissues. The difference in outcome is interesting.

Discuss

- What will you use?
- What measurements will you need?
- How will you fix the box together?
- What shapes will you need to cut out?
- How will you make sure the box is strong enough? big enough?

Teachers may prefer to change this activity so that the children are expected to make a container which will hold ten of something, e.g. conkers, bowlfuls of cereal, oranges, children, balloons, cubes, grains of rice, etc.

• Using and Applying Mathematics	2a;3a,c
• Shape, Space and Measures	4a,b,c

11   PARCELS

LENGTH, VOLUME, WEIGHT

Parcels are only allowed through the post if the length plus width plus depth is less than 1.85 metres. Find some boxes and sort them according to which can and which cannot be posted.

Teachers may choose to make the activity simpler by reducing the maximum value of the dimensions to 50 centimetres.

This activity gives children experience of the relationship between the dimensions of a box and its volume.

Before they start

The children need to be able to measure with reasonable accuracy, add linear measurements and to measure volumes and weights using standard and non-standard measures.

Discuss

- Are you good at guessing which ones can and cannot be posted?
- What is the narrowest/tallest/widest/strangest box you have found that can be posted?

- Did any of the boxes surprise you?
- Which of your boxes that can be posted will hold the most?
- How are you keeping a record of the dimensions?
- How will you find out how much each of them will hold?
- Could you make a box which has dimensions which measure exactly 1.85 (or 0.5) metres?

•	Using and Applying Mathematics	2c;4b,d
•	Shape, Space and Measures	4a,b,c

12   HOW MANY VITAL STATISTICS CAN YOU FIND OUT ABOUT YOUR BODY?

LENGTH, AREA, VOLUME
This activity gives children experience of estimating and measuring length and area, and of measuring curved surfaces.

Before they start

The children will need to discuss the fact that everyone is different and that different kinds of measurement are possible, i.e. not only linear measures. They might choose to measure: head size, face size, biceps size and strength, total finger measurement, type of finger and toe print, area of hand and foot prints, leg length compared with height, height, weight, surface area, sitting height, kneeling height, jumping height, reach, stride, span, strength by pushing scales or squeezing a bottle.

Discuss

- Which measures are easiest to take?
- What is the best/easiest way to record what you have found?
- Could you make a model of yourself from cylinders?
- Can you find any relationships? E.g. How many smiles equal your height? How many fingers equal your reach?
- Can you find parts of you which are half, quarter and third your height?
- Would it be helpful to use a computer? How might you use it?

•	Using and Applying Mathematics	2b;3b;4a
•	Shape, Space and Measures	4a,b,c

13 DOES YOUR CHAIR FIT YOU?

LENGTH

Why do some people have a favourite chair?

This activity gives children experience of linear measure in context.

Before they start

Without moving out of their chairs, ask the children to estimate the following:

- the height of their chair (floor to back);
- the distance from their own head to their own seat;
- the distance from the seat of the chair to the floor;
- their own knee-to-floor measurement;
- their chair seat length;
- their own seat-to-knee measurement.

Then ask them to measure.

Discuss

- What would be the dimensions of the ideal chair for you?
- If you were a chair manufacturer, what size chairs would you build to suit as many people as possible? (The children will need to do some research to answer this question thoroughly.)

• Using and Applying Mathematics	3c;4b,c
• Shape, Space and Measures	4a,b

14 MAKE A TRUNDLE WHEEL

LENGTH

This activity gives children experience of relating a linear length to a curved one, and of using a trundle wheel as a measuring device.

Before they start

The children need to have measured in non-standard units of measure and maybe with metres. It will also be useful if a commercially produced trundle wheel can be used as a visual aid. Ask the children to choose a body measure to make into a trundle wheel. For example, body length, reach, step, span, arm length.

Discuss

- How will you make your trundle wheel the right size? (They may choose to take a string measurement and make that piece of string into a circle or, if they know all about circumferences, they may calculate the diameter of the circle.)
- What will you make your wheel with?
- What will you use your wheel to measure?
- Devise some questions so someone else can use your wheel. Compare the trundle wheels with other wheels, bicycle wheels, push chair wheels, model car wheels, etc.

•	Using and Applying Mathematics	2c,d;3a
•	Shape, Space and Measures	4a,b

15   HOW FAR AWAY CAN YOU SEE A MOUSE?

LENGTH
This activity gives children experience of setting up a vision test, measuring, and collecting and recording data.

Before they start

The children need to discuss whether or not using a real mouse would be a good idea, and at what increments of distance they need to test to see the mouse. They also need to be able to measure in metres or some other relatively large non-standard unit of measure.

Discuss

- Do you need to test every 10 centimetres? How far then?
- How will you record your findings?
- Does it make a difference what colour/how big the mouse is?
- How could you test hearing and smell? Will the best hearers also be the best smellers?
- Would a computer database be helpful to sort out the information?

•	Using and Applying Mathematics	2c;3b,c
•	Shape, Space and Measures	4a,b

16   MAKE A BAG TO CARRY 5 KILOGRAMS

LENGTH, AREA, CAPACITY, WEIGHT
This activity gives children experience of actually handling
5 kilograms, and helps them to understand how strong something
has to be to carry such a weight.

Before they start

The children all need to have plenty of time to handle the
5 kilograms, to give them a feeling for what they are up against in
this task, and to look at a variety of bags and consider their
construction. They also need to know how to make newspaper
strong, i.e. by rolling or folding, or by using lots of layers.

Discuss

- What size should the bag be?
- How will you make the bag strong enough?
- How will you test the bags when they are finished?
- How would you make different bags for different weights?
- What would the best material be to make it from?
- How will you make the handles?
- Does a shopping bag normally need to hold this weight?

• Using and Applying Mathematics	2a,b,c
• Shape, Space and Measures	4a,b,c

17   INVENT A NEW WAY OF MEASURING

LENGTH, AREA, CAPACITY/VOLUME, TIME, WEIGHT
This activity gives children experience of discussing the need for
standard measures and of choosing appropriate units.

Before they start

The children need to have had some experience of comparison and
ordering within the area of measure they are considering, and, in
particular, measuring in non-standard units.

Discuss

- What will you use to measure with? (E.g. for Area, they could use egg boxes, so a space might measure four boxes and two egg spaces.)
- What do you want to measure with it?
- How will you make a ruler? (E.g. ten buttons on a ruler or string with a knot tied every finger length.)
- How will you test your measuring system?

•	Using and Applying Mathematics	2a,d;3a
•	Shape, Space and Measures	4a,b,c

18   MAKE A STRIP OF PAPER 1 KILOMETRE LONG

LENGTH
You might prefer to make it 10 metres!
   This activity gives children experience of accurate measures and the relationship between units of measurement.

Before they start

The children will need to have used metres and to have discussed the relationship between metres, centimetres and kilometres.

Discuss

- How will you keep track of the length of your strip?
- How wide will you make it?
- What will you make it from?
- How will you organise yourselves?

When they have finished:

- If you were going to do this again, would you work differently?

•	Using and Applying Mathematics	2c,d;3a
•	Shape, Space and Measures	4a,b

19 PLAN A TRIP

CAPACITY, WEIGHT, TIME

This activity gives children experience of costing, budgeting time, and quantity. This is largely a measurement decision-making process, with the main assumption being that the trip is connected with measurement or your current topic.

Before they start

The children may need to have been involved in less ambitious projects, such as planning the timetable.

Discuss

- Where shall we go?
- How long do we need to be there for?
- How will we travel?
- How long will the journey take?
- How shall we spend the time that we are there?
- How shall we let your parents know?
- What will we need to take? What will we eat?
- Do we need spending money while we are there?
- How much will the trip cost?

• Using and Applying Mathematics	2a,c;3c
• Shape, Space and Measures	4a,b

20 PLAN A PICNIC

CAPACITY, WEIGHT, TIME

This activity gives children experience of researching preferred food, estimating and calculating quantities.

Before they start

The children may need to have been involved in less ambitious projects, such as planning the timetable.

Discuss

- How much space will we need for us all to sit down?
- How will we decide what to take? How much drink will we need?

- How much shall we spend?
- Do we need crockery and cutlery?
- Reflect on the picnic; did we have enough? too much?
- Did we spend too much?
- Was it a healthy meal?

• Using and Applying Mathematics	2a,b,c
• Shape, Space and Measures	4a,b

21   PLAN A BRING-AND-BUY SALE

CAPACITY, WEIGHT, TIME
This activity gives children experience of using money, costing and valuing.

Before they start

The children need to be able to recognise coins, give change and calculate small amounts of money with and/or without a calculator.

Discuss

- What sort of things will sell best?
- Should we bring things from home or make things for the sale?
- How can you decide what to charge? (Children may need to research this.)
- Who will we sell to? Mums and dads? Other children? Older children?
- What will we use the money for?
- How shall we arrange the room?
- How much space will we need?
- Reflect on the activity; could we now organise another sale which runs more smoothly and makes more money than the first?!

• Using and Applying Mathematics	2b,c;4d
• Shape, Space and Measures	4a,b

22   MAKE A CLOCK

LENGTH, VOLUME, TIME

This activity gives children experience of timing and measuring lengths and volumes and areas and relating them.

Before they start

The children need to be aware of what a clock does and to have had substantial discussion about the different clocks that have been used throughout history, e.g. water clocks, candle clocks, sand clocks, pendulums, sundials.

Discuss

- What type of clock will you make?

PENDULUMS
- How will you make it last longer?
- Can you make each swing last exactly one second?
- Try longer string... shorter string... wider/narrower swings, heavier and lighter weights.

WATER CLOCKS
- Which containers will you use?
- How will you make the water/sand travel slowly?
- Can you make it last more than one minute? five minutes?
- Can you change it so you can use it to tell the time?

SUNDIALS
- What is the best shape?
- What will you use to cast a shadow?
- How will you use it to tell the time?

• Using and Applying Mathematics	2d;3a;4c
• Shape, Space and Measures	4a,b,c

23   MAKE A HAT

LENGTH, AREA

This activity gives children experience of choosing appropriate units of measure, taking reasonably accurate measurements and allowing for overlaps.

Before they start

The children need the chance to look at a variety of hats and how they might be made, and to be able to measure in some way.

Discuss

- What type of hat will you make?
- What will you make it from?
- How much do you think you will need?
- What shape(s) will you cut out?
- How can you be sure it will fit?
- How will you fix it together?

• Using and Applying Mathematics		2a,b,c
• Shape, Space and Measures		4a,b,c

24 HOW MUCH SPACE DOES YOUR SKIN TAKE UP?

LENGTH, AREA

This activity gives children experience of choosing and using appropriate units of measurement. To find the solution, they may need to wrap themselves in paper, plasticine or cloth. (Alternatively, let the children find the area of the clothes they are wearing.)

Before they start

The children need to have experience of using units of measure suitable to their development, square decimetres, square centimetres, square metres or a non-standard measure (the question can be changed to suit the unit, e.g. 'If someone walked all over you, how many footsteps would they need?). They may also need to have access to a means of calculating measurements.

Discuss

- How much skin do you think you have? Enough to cover the floor, your desk?
- Could you use anything to help you find out?
- Will both arms be the same?
- Do we need to know exactly?

• Using and Applying Mathematics		2c;3c;4a
• Shape, Space and Measures		4a,b,c

25   HOW MUCH WALLPAPER WOULD YOU NEED TO DECORATE THE SCHOOL?

LENGTH, AREA

This activity gives children experience of using and calculating areas and lengths.

Before they start

The children need to know:

- what a square metre is;
- how wallpaper is sold;
- that patterns on wallpaper need to be matched up;
- that you cannot join a sheet of wallpaper halfway up the wall;
- that an exact measurement is not necessary;
- that least waste is preferable.

Discuss

- Will every strip be complete? Can we use the spare bits? All of them?
- Do we need to measure exactly? How can we estimate?
- How can we make the estimate more precise?
- How much glass? wood? paint? do you think would be needed for your classroom?
- How many strips would you get from one roll? Which way round do you stick it?
- Does every piece you stick need to be as tall as the room?

• Using and Applying Mathematics		2b,c,d
• Shape, Space and Measures		4a,b,c

26   TEN METRES OF STRING

LENGTH, AREA

Make a knot to mark every metre and use it to measure. This activity gives children experience of comparing area and perimeter and of using a very long ruler.

Before they start

The children need to have done some measuring using non-standard measures in length and area.

Discuss

- What would it be sensible to use your ruler for? Set some challenges for each other.
- How accurate can you be with your giant ruler?
- How many steps fit along your ruler? How many children? How many chairs? tables? snakes?

Use 1 metre to make a circle shape.

- How many children will fit inside?
- Try two metres. Three metres. Can you predict?

•	Using and Applying Mathematics	2a;3a;4d
•	Shape, Space and Measures	4a,b,c

27 POLYOMINOES

LENGTH, PERIMETER, AREA
This activity gives children experience of comparing perimeter and area.

Before they start

The children need to know what a perimeter is and to have some understanding of square units of area.

Ask the children to use a collection of identical squares for this activity. They will need to choose a number of squares to investigate, e.g. six. Ask them to arrange the squares in as many different ways as they can. Ask them to find the area and perimeter of each one.

Discuss

- Do any have the same perimeter?
- Can you predict what the perimeter is likely to be?
- What is the greatest/least perimeter you can make?
- Can you make all the numbers in between the greatest and least?
- What might happen if you tried a different number of squares? Try to find out.
- Try other shapes, e.g. equilateral triangles, regular hexagons.

•	Using and Applying Mathematics	3a,c;4b
•	Shape, Space and Measures	4a,b,c

APPENDIX: PROGRAMMES OF STUDY REFERENCE CHARTS

SHAPE, SPACE AND MEASURES: KEY STAGE 1

3 Understanding and using properties of position and movement	4 Understanding and using measures

a   describe positions, using common words; recognise movements in a straight line, i.e. translation, and rotations, and combine them in simple ways; copy, continue and make patterns.
 	
Flowers
Towers
Turn!
Letters
	a compare objects and events using appropriate language, by direct comparison, and then using common non-standard and standard units of length, mass and capacity, e.g. 'three-and-a-bit metres long', 'as heavy as ten conkers', 'about three beakers' full'; begin to use a wider range of standard units, including standard units of time, choosing units appropriate to a situation; estimate with these units.
	
	Length
	   Beads
	   Ten
	   Sorting box
	   How long?
	   Plasticine sausages
	   Bodies
	   Detectives
	   Make a line
	
	Mass
	   Filling boxes
	   Kilogram collections
	   Plasticine models
	   Envelopes
	
	Capacity/Volume
	   Paint
	   Fill a pot
	   Sinkers
	   Junk boxes
	   Body parts
	
	Time
	   Take your time
	   Modelling
	   Days of the week
	   Busy times
	   Time lines
	   A big clock
	   Clock patience
	
	Area
	   Covering boxes
	   Body prints
	   Body measures
	   Cotton wool balls
	   Vegetables
	   Shadows
	   Boxes
	   Letter shapes

b understand angle as a measure of turn and recognise quarter turns and half turns, e.g. giving instructions for rotating a programmable toy; recognise right angles. *Turn! Letters*	b choose and use simple measuring instruments, reading and interpreting numbers and scales with some accuracy. **Time** *A big clock Clock patience*

SHAPE, SPACE AND MEASURES: KEY STAGE 2

3 Understanding and using properties of position and movement	4 Understanding and using measures
c use right angles, fractions of a turn and, later, degrees, to measure rotation, and use the associated language. *Make two circles*	a **choose appropriate standard units of length** *Metre mouse* *How high?* Make a giant ant, spider or bird to scale Make a model of the school Make a map of your classroom How much water will fill up the classroom? How much does your house weigh? Make a box to hold 1 kilogram Parcels How many vital statistics can you find out about your body? Does your chair fit you? Make a trundle wheel How far away can you see a mouse? Make a bag to carry 5 kilograms Invent a new way of measuring Make a clock Make a hat How much space does your skin take up? Ten metres of string How much wallpaper would you need to decorate the school? Polyominoes **mass** *Weigh yourself* *Popcorn* *How many stones?* *Gravel balance* *Magnets* Make a set of weights How much does your house weigh? Does the class weigh a tonne? Make a box to hold 1 kilogram Parcels Make a bag to carry 5 kilograms Invent a new way of measuring Plan a trip Plan a picnic Plan a bring-and-buy sale **capacity** *Sponges* *Blanket box* *Elastic bands* *Fill a litre* 200 grams of plasticine How much water will fill up the classroom? How much do you drink in a day? Dripping tap Make a bag to carry 5 kilograms Invent a new way of measuring Plan a trip Plan a picnic Plan a bring-and-buy sale **time** *Jar lids* *Digital display* *How long did it take?*

How much do you drink in a day?
Dripping tap
Invent a new way of measuring
Plan a trip
Plan a picnic
Plan a bring-and-buy sale
Make a clock

and make sensible estimates with them in everyday situations;
How high?
Weigh yourself
Popcorn
How many stones?
Magnets
Sponges
Blanket box
Elastic bands
Fill a litre
Grids
Make square metre
Make a giant ant, spider or bird to scale
Make a model of the school
How much water will fill up the classroom?
Make a set of weights
How much does your house weigh?
How much do you drink in a day?
Dripping tap
Does the class weigh a tonne?
Make a box to hold 1 kilogram
Parcels
How many vital statistics can you find out about your body?
Does your chair fit you?
Make a trundle wheel
How far away can you see a mouse?
Make a bag to carry 5 kilograms
Invent a new way of measuring
Plan a trip
Plan a picnic
Plan a bring-and-buy sale
Make a clock
Make a hat
How much space does your skin take up?
How much wallpaper would you need to decorate the school?
Ten metres of string
Polyominoes

extend their understanding of the relationship between units
Metre mouse
How high?
Weigh yourself
Popcorn
How many stones?
Gravel balance
Magnets
Blanket box
Elastic bands
Fill a litre
Jar lids
How long did it take?
Digital display
Grids
Make a square metre
Make a giant ant, spider or bird to scale
How much water will fill up the classroom?
Make a set of weights

How much does your house weigh?
How much do you drink in a day?
Dripping tap
Does the class weigh a tonne?
Make a box to hold 1 kilogram
Parcels
How many vital statistics can you find out about your body?
Does your chair fit you?
Make a trundle wheel
How far away can you see a mouse?
Make a bag to carry 5 kilograms
Invent a new way of measuring
Plan a trip
Plan a picnic
Plan a bring-and-buy sale
Make a clock
Make a hat
How much space does your skin take up?
How much wallpaper would you need to decorate the school?
Ten metres of string
Polyominoes

convert one metric unit to another
How high?
Weigh yourself
Popcorn
How many stones?
Gravel balance
Magnets
Elastic bands
Fill a litre
200 grams of plasticine
Digital display
Make a giant ant, spider or bird to scale
Make a model of the school
How much water will fill up the classroom?
Make a set of weights
How much does your house weigh?
How much do you drink in a day?
Dripping tap
Does the class weigh a tonne?
Make a box to hold 1 kilogram
Parcels
How many vital statistics can you find out about your body?
Does your chair fit you?
Make a trundle wheel
How far away can you see a mouse?
Make a bag to carry 5 kilograms
Invent a new way of measuring
Plan a trip
Plan a picnic
Plan a bring-and-buy sale
Make a clock
Make a hat
How much space does your skin take up?
How much wallpaper would you need to decorate the school?
Ten metres of string
Polyominoes

know the rough metric equivalents of imperial units still in daily use
Weigh yourself
Popcorn
Magnets

b choose and use appropriate measuring instruments

Make two circles
How high?
Weigh yourself
Popcorn
How many stones?
Gravel balance
Magnets
Elastic bands
Fill a litre
200 grams of plasticine
Guess which box
Jar lids
How long did it take?
Grids
Make a square metre
Make a giant ant, spider or bird to scale
Make a model of the school
How much water will fill up the classroom?
Make a set of weights
How much does your house weigh?
How much do you drink in a day?
Dripping tap
Does the class weigh a tonne?
Make a box to hold 1 kilogram
Parcels
How many vital statistics can you find out about your body?
Does your chair fit you?
Make a trundle wheel
How far away can you see a mouse?
Make a bag to carry 5 kilograms
Invent a new way of measuring
Plan a trip
Plan a picnic
Plan a bring-and-buy sale
Make a clock
Make a hat
How much space does your skin take up?
How much wallpaper would you need to decorate the school?
Ten metres of string
Polyominoes

interpret numbers and read scales to an increasing degree of accuracy

Metre mouse
How high?
Weigh yourself
Popcorn
How many stones?
Gravel balance
Magnets
Elastic bands
Fill a litre
200 grams of plasticine
Guess which box
Jar lids
How long did it take?
Digital display
Make a giant ant, spider or bird to scale
Make a model of the school
How much water will fill up the classroom?
Make a set of weights
How much does your house weigh?
How much do you drink in a day?

Dripping tap
Does the class weigh a tonne?
Make a box to hold 1 kilogram
Parcels
How many vital statistics can you find out about your body?
Does your chair fit you?
Make a trundle wheel
How far away can you see a mouse?
Make a bag to carry 5 kilograms
Invent a new way of measuring
Plan a trip
Plan a picnic
Plan a bring-and-buy sale
Make a clock
Make a hat
How much space does your skin take up?
How much wallpaper would you need to decorate the school?
Ten metres of string
Polyominoes

c find perimeters of simple shapes
Polyominoes

find practically the circumferences of circles, being introduced to the ratio pi

find areas by counting methods, leading to the use of other practical methods, e.g. dissection
Guess which box
Covering boxes
Body prints
Body measures
Cotton wool balls
Vegetables
Boxes
Letter shapes
Grids
Make a square metre
Make a giant ant, spider or bird to scale
Make a model of the school
How much water will fill up the classroom?
How much does your house weigh?
How many vital statistics can you find out about your body?
Make a bag to carry 5 kilograms
Invent a new way of measuring
Polyominoes

find volumes by counting methods, leading to the use of other practical methods, e.g. dissection
How much water will fill up the classroom?
Make a set of weights
How much does your house weigh?
Make a box to hold 1 kilogram
Parcels
How many vital statistics can you find out about your body?
Invent a new way of measuring
Make a clock

USING AND APPLYING MATHEMATICS: KEY STAGE 1

Pupils should be taught to:		
2 Making and monitoring decisions to solve problems	**3 Developing mathematical language and communication**	**4 Solving numerical problems**
a select and use the appropriate mathematics *A big clock*	a understand the language of number, properties of shapes and comparatives, e.g. 'bigger than', 'next to', 'before' *Beads* *Sorting box* *Plasticine sausages* *Detectives* *Plasticine models* *Envelopes* *Fill a pot* *Vegetables* *Sinkers* *Junk boxes* *Take your time* *Modelling* *Busy times* *Days of the week* *Covering boxes*	a recognise simple patterns and relationships and make related predictions about them
b select and use mathematical equipment and materials *Filling boxes* *Kilogram collections* *Body prints* *Body measures*	b relate numerals and other mathematical symbols, e.g. '+', '=', to a range of situations	b ask questions including 'What would happen if?' and 'Why?', e.g. considering the behaviour of a programmable toy *Towers* *Turn!*
c develop different mathematical approaches and look for ways to overcome difficulties *Ten* *Make a line* *Paint*	c discuss their work, responding to and asking mathematical questions *How long?* *Time lines* *Letter shapes*	c understand general statements, e.g. 'all even numbers divide by 2', and investigate whether particular cases match them
d organise and check their work *Flowers* *Clock patience* *Shadows*	d use a variety of forms of mathematical presentation *Bodies* *Cotton wool balls* *Boxes*	

USING AND APPLYING MATHEMATICS: KEY STAGE 2

Pupils should be taught to:

2 Making and monitoring decisions to solve problems	3 Developing mathematical language and communication	4 Solving numerical problems
a select and use the appropriate mathematics and materials *Metre mouse* *Blanket box* *Make a square metre* Make a model of the school How much water will fill up the classroom? Make a box to hold 1 kilogram Make a bag to carry 5 kilograms Invent a new way of measuring Plan a trip Plan a picnic Make a hat Ten metres of string	a understand and use the language of: • number; • the properties and movements of shapes; • measures; • simple probability • relationships, including 'multiple of', 'factor of' and 'symmetrical to' *Doors* *Gravel balance* *200 grams of plasticine* *Digital display* Make a giant ant, spider or bird to scale Make a model of the school Make a set of weights How much does your house weigh? Does the class weigh a tonne? Make a box to hold 1 kilogram Make a trundle wheel Make a strip of paper 1 kilometre long Invent a new way of measuring Make a clock Ten metres of string Polyominoes	a understand and investigate general statements, e.g. 'wrist size is half neck size', 'there are four prime numbers less than 10' How many vital statistics can you find out about your body? How much space does your skin take up?
b try different mathematical approaches; identify and obtain information needed to carry out their work *How many stones?* *Guess which box* *Cones* Make a map of your classroom How much do you drink in a day? How many vital statistics can you find out about your body? Make a bag to carry 5 kilograms Plan a picnic Make a hat Plan a bring-and-buy sale How much wallpaper would you need to decorate the school?	b use diagrams, graphs and simple algebraic symbols Make a map of your classroom How many vital statistics can you find out about your body? Dripping tap How far away can you see a mouse?	b search for pattern in their results Make a giant ant, spider or bird to scale How much water will fill up the classroom? Make a set of weights How much do you drink in a day? Parcels Does your chair fit you? Polyominoes
c develop their own mathematical strategies and look for ways to overcome difficulties *Elastic bands* *Fill a litre* *Cones* *Floor plans* *How long did it take?* *Grids* Make a giant ant, spider or bird to scale How much does your house weigh? Does the class weigh a tonne? Make a box to hold 1 kilogram Parcels Make a trundle wheel How far away can you see a mouse? Make a strip of paper 1 kilometre long Make a bag to carry 5 kilograms Plan a trip Plan a picnic Plan a bring-and-buy sale Make a hat How much wallpaper would you need to decorate the school?	c present information and results clearly, and explain the reasons for their choice of presentation *How high?* *Sponges* Make a set of weights Does your chair fit you? How far away can you see a mouse? Plan a trip How much space does your skin take up? Polyominoes	c make general statements of their own, based on evidence they have produced Dripping tap Does your chair fit you? Make a clock
d check their results and consider whether they are reasonable *Weigh yourself* *Popcorn* *Jar lids* Make a model of the school Make a map of your classroom How much does your house weigh? How much do you drink in a day? Does the class weigh a tonne? Make a trundle wheel Make a strip of paper 1 kilometre long Invent a new way of measuring Make a clock How much wallpaper would you need to decorate the school?		d explain their reasoning *Magnets* How much water will fill up the classroom? Dripping tap Parcels Plan a bring-and-buy sale Ten metres of string

GLOSSARY

calibrate put marks on to indicate a scale

Carroll diagram a way of representing information invented by Lewis Carroll (see figure 67)

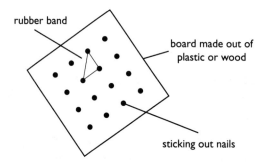

FIGURE 67 *Carroll diagram*

centilitre one-hundredth of a litre

circumference the linear distance around the edge of a circle

geoboards a pinboard with pins arranged as in figure 68

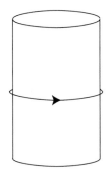

FIGURE 68 *Geoboard*

girth the distance around a three-dimensional shape (see figure 69)

Inset giver someone who runs a training course for teachers (**In-S**ervice **T**raining)

logo a computer language with an excellent graphics facility

millilitre one-thousandth of a litre

FIGURE 69 *Girth*

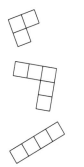

polydron flat shapes which join together to make three-dimensional models

polyominoes shapes made from any number of squares which are joined along their sides (see figure 70)

Roamer a programmable robotic toy which children can direct to move forwards, backwards and to turn through a specified number of degrees

scalene shapes polygons with no symmetry

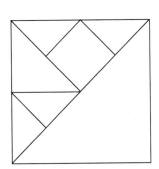

FIGURE 70 *Polyominoes*

tangram a Chinese shape puzzle

tree diagram a way of representing information (see figure 72)

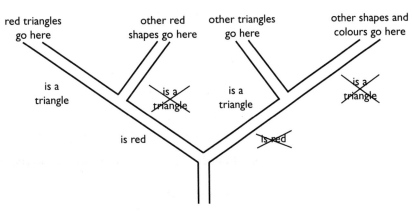

FIGURE 71 *Tangram*

FIGURE 72 *Tree diagram*

trundle wheel a wheel on a stick with a circumference of 1 metre, used to measure distance. As it turns, it clicks every time it passes a metre.

Venn diagram a way of representing information (see figure 73)

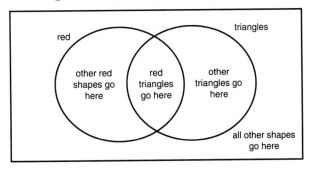

FIGURE 73 *Venn diagram*